Habits Driven

Is the

Game Changer

By Joe Siau

~

Fast Productions

Straight Arrow Publications

Copyright 2022

Acknowledgments

Nothing would be possible if this book were only all about me. Instead, it is about #MeToWe. Countless individuals have played memorable roles in my life. With each journey along the way, my borrowers, realtors, and referring partners encouraged me repeatedly. Thank you!

Thank you: Dad, Mom, Esther, John, Grace, Marina, Stephanie, Jeremy, Monette Howell, Carlton Sue, Richard Doughty, Phil Parham, Garrett Mock, John Howarth, Diane Bacon, Janine Romney, Felicia Bowers, CCM, The Southwestern Company, and The Homeowners Financial Group. Thank you for your tremendous amount of support and friendship over the years! By divine design, you were instrumental for me to tell my story.

After attending a seminar promoted by Tom Daves with Brent Gove, I felt inspired to author this book. Writing is a mindset, just like the habit is a mindset when others may make excuses. And if I couldn't write the first draft of my book in 30 days, how could I teach others about mindset and habits, right?

"We are what we repeatedly do. Excellence then is not an act but a habit." – *Aristotle*

Foreword

As long as I have known Joe, he has been very results-oriented! I was fortunate to recruit Joe as a college student to sell books door to door for the Southwestern Publishing company while he attended USC. He met me in Nashville, TN, and agreed to sell books 80 hours a week on the east coast for the summer. He not only finished as a top salesman for the company, but his leadership skills were also incredible for the next two years. Joe worked hard, studied the sales material, and was incredibly teachable. His character is impeccable. Joe had clocked in at least 3,000 hours in the book field, and he is a subject matter expert in human nature, getting results, and a great marketer. Thirty-eight years later, I had no doubt Joe would be an impressive family man, have a successful career, and is a pillar in his community. The details and examples Joe shared in this book will profoundly affect YOU when you read every word to the end. His book will read like a Tom Clancy novel; action-packed! Get ready for some life-changing perspectives – *Monette Howell-Sedberry*

I have such a passion for people who are successful through grit! Love your faith and perseverance – *Janine Romney*

Habits Driven
Is the Game Changer
Five Events that Altered My Life
Table of Contents

Preface

Year after year, I donated money to numerous charities. That's like giving someone a fish. So, when you read this book, you may agree that this book is like showing someone how to fish, like a Think and Grow Rich book.

I hope this book will get into the hands of all the foster kids currently going through the Court Appointed Child Advocate (CASA) program, where foster kids can see patterns of someone working hard, putting in the long hours, and when working hard has its merits and its rewards. Also, I hope this book gets into the hands of all those going through prison correction reform or kids who are raised by single parents, or for you, if you are struggling in life with addiction, or if you are homeless, or you have been abandoned mothers at Acres of Hope. Finally, I hope this book will also fall into the hands of foster kids connected to Compassion Planet, an agency that helps local Foster Youth aging out of the system with job skills. Sometimes, kids in their teens or adults just need more than a basketball player or a pop artist as their role model, right?

I feel honored and privileged to share my life stories and ideas with you and impart the terms and conditions of developing good habits, all of which you must learn while you're young or as early as possible. I based these habits on repeatedly doing many activities in a brief period so one day, it will miraculously replicate itself into your future patterns of success, no matter how upside down your future may get.

Preface

The next generation sometimes is more important. The fabric of our country rests on how parents lead kids to become responsible teenagers. As young adults, what and who shapes their thinking and behaviors? How can I be involved instead of just donating?

How do you or your kids go from Point A to Point B with better odds of success? What ideas do you have; what habits will keep you on track? We are all unique individuals. Everyone possesses the ability to acquire some level of success by luck. Some may shortcut their struggles even further by studying for success. This book is about the latter.

Habits are nothing more than consistent patterns repeated. To me, they are repeated in my stories as 20 minutes consistently, 30-day or 90-day habits, or over three years habits that kept repeating over and over. These have been my winning patterns or losing patterns.

"We first make our habits, and then our habits make us" – *John Dryden*

This book is not for those thinking of being a doctor, dentist, lawyer, computer programmer or engineer, or someone who wants to work at Google, Facebook, or in the political field. But, this would be an excellent foundation for those trying to be an actor, an athlete, or running a self-employed business, business venture, or sales. This book would also be an excellent resource for parents or teachers giving their kids or students tools for reflection.

This book is not about 10X scaling a business; it's not about Think and Grow Rich; it could be better than that.

Sometimes, it is through seeing the similarities or the differences in others that one gains a better unique perspective on how to execute ideas in your unique way, which helps you live by developing better patterns and habits.

My story may not be your story. Your plan and strategies may be different than mine. Many have excelled due to vast struggles, adversity, health conditions, injuries, or the death of a loved one. I did not have good business relationship skills. Some have great successes based on solid business relationship skills built over decades. I was not good-looking, not gregarious, and did not have the gift of the gab. Some have more significant successes with their refined people skills and charismatic nature; I applaud you for a head start and your accomplishments as we continue our journeys together from:

Faith --> Habit --> Ideas --> Bending --> Change --> Faith

Not:
Denial --> Anger --> Bargaining --> Depression --> Acceptance

"Habits Driven is the Game Changer"
Habits will help you build muscle memories

Forming Lifelong Habits

Chapter One

Where do you learn how to build good habits?

I started studying Electrical Engineering at USC. It was so hard. It didn't come easy, especially with eight hours of USC Trojans Marching Band practice per week, and the Saturdays wiped me out after performing at the football game all day. Then I switched to industrial engineering with my friend, who also struggled in Electrical Engineering. After my sophomore year at USC, I went home for the summer. I found jobs as a busboy at the Charlie Brown Restaurant chain at night and worked as a Kelly Girl temporary typist for Lawrence Berkeley Laboratory during the day. No extraordinarily significant events happened there, and I did not learn or take away much.

One day, I received a postcard about how to make more money in the summertime. Of course, I responded, and two days later, I received this call from Monett from Oregon. When was the last time you picked up a phone call, and that call changed your life?

"Hi Joe, this is Monett Howell. Your postcard response indicates that you are attending USC and studying engineering. Did you know that many engineers fail in their careers if they don't have people skills? Harvard came out with a study where 85% of your successes are based on your people skills, not your technical skills. So, here's what you need to do. I have a group of college students coming to meet me."

"I will give you the names and addresses of these students at Santa Clara University. Then, can you ask your father to drive you to Santa Clara University?" I said OK, but what do I do?

Monet continued, "They will carpool you to Santa Barbara and meet up with other college students there. Then you will carpool to Cal Poly to meet other college students. Then you'll sleep a night there, drive across the country to Nashville and come to a sales school training with me."

"It would be a one-week sales school training; you don't need to pay anything. We will teach you how to make money selling books door to door and pay your way through college."

Monett said, "Joe, if you work hard, study hard, and are teachable, yet you don't like what you learn, I will buy a plane ticket to fly you back after training. If you like what you learned, then I want you to commit to working with me. Come hell or high water; you must stick it through for the rest of the summer with me, OK?"

I responded, "I will check with my dad to see if I can sell books with you this summer." I was surprised when my dad said yes.

I then called Monett back to confirm, which was the 2nd event that changed my life. The first was my father, who immigrated from our family to the US.

We arrived in Nashville on a Sunday, ate, slept, and went to the Southwestern Company Sales School on a Monday with like a thousand other college students from across the United States. We heard past Sales Managers speak and motivational speakers Dennis Waitley and Og Mangdino speak in person.

I learned about the seven cycles of sales:

1. pre-approaching
2. approaching
3. establishing rapport
4. introduction
5. demonstration
6. answering objections
7. collecting cash

After putting it on paper at the end of the summer, I even got two college credits for what I had learned as an elective. Oops, that gave it away. No, I didn't quit. I didn't fly home when sales school finished. However, I had to give up watching the 1984 Summer Olympic performances at Los Angeles and USC. Some of my friends went, but I wanted something more in my life, so I chose to give up not watching the 1984 Olympics.

Selling Books Door to Door

I learned how to be habits-driven daily when selling books door to door.

When sales school ended, my team and I were assigned to go to Asheboro, NC. Finally, after seven hours of driving, we got to Asheboro at night; we were ready.

They trained our team in the following manner:

A dollar bill was placed on the toilet to see who would be first to grab the dollar at 6:59 in the morning. The first morning I slept in enabled my roommate Bede to beat me to it. Then we would go to grab breakfast at the same diner each morning. We all ordered the same special each morning.

After breakfast, we danced in front of the restaurant to our crazy song, "It's a Great Day to be a Bookman, It's the Best Thing I Know." From then on, we knocked on our first door at 7:59 am every morning. Bede and I were on our bikes, and Steve drove through the country roads in his car.

Every morning, afternoon, and evening, I would knock on doors; automatically, I took three steps back and turned to my side. This way, I did not appear threatening when the door opened. Then, I would wait and pause until the lady said something. I would then turn and step backward to create additional non-threatening space.

First, I smiled (which often, I would forget), then repetitively, I would say: "Hi, Mrs. Jones, I'm Joe Siau from California. I'm one of those college students working in this area, talking to all the families with kids going to the XXX elementary school. I was talking to your neighbor Mrs. Johnson with Jenny and Susie in first and third grades; you know them, right? Do you have a place where we can sit down?"

Repeatedly, I initiated, pre-approached, and approached (with my nerdy engineering analytical thinking). I forced myself to smile (which, most every day, I was not feeling it). I established rapport (with a canned script), and I would ask the same trained rhetorical questions to break the ice. "As I said, I'm from California. "Have you ever been there? The weather here is surely different; how do you put up with the mosquitos out here? They're almost the size of a chicken. Haha 😊."

Then with another memorized scripted introduction, I invite the kids to come in. Then I recited the product demonstration script that I had regurgitated a hundred times. Then I would start closing. Oops, they raised a question; wait, was that a question or was that an objection? OK, I would power through with Objection Answer #3 this time, or #4 would work better. I wouldn't say I like #5 cause it's too cheesy. Dang! I don't quite remember how to use Objection Answer #6. Greenlight, then I begin the collecting cash script, or I would go to the next door and repeat this process all over again, talking to another family with kids.

From Engineer Minded to Developing People Skills

I would make 30 sales presentations per day at 20 minutes apart. That's 30 scripted, memorized presentations per day. That meant I worked from 7:59 am to 10 pm. I worked six days a week. After one week, I would have made over 180 x 20 minutes of sales presentations. I learned that incremental successes build confidence. Then by running between homes, I had no time to think about whether the family said yes or no. I became a machine, and my goal was to provide educational service to folks whether they liked it or not. When I let go of my fears, doubts, needing to make money, the friends back home, drinking on the beach; and my single-minded purpose of serving my community and providing an educational product, I was not distracted by the yeses or the noes. I went from one door to the next, continuing that process for ten weeks in my first year's summer.

In my first year, I spoke to over 5,000 families and sat down with over 1800 families. I gave them presentations on how the study guides and books would be usable for the kids when computers were not popular. They taught me to be service-minded rather than making it about me. It was all about showing the benefit of my books and how they would benefit their children throughout their school years. When I focused on others, my results continued to improve.

My approach was, "Mrs. Jones, on some Christmas, when your kids pull out these Study Guides as you sit by the fireplace, and you see them looking up facts on a President to answer a trivia question or looking for facts for their math homework, you won't regret how much you paid for these books, will you? They taught us the script to use to close the sale. We did not wait for their yes or no. We just moved on after that.

Sunday meetings were a blast. College students working 2-3 hours away would drive in, and we would congregate in a hotel for our Sunday meetings. Everyone had great sales stories or battle scars to share. We were not alone. We all helped each other. Then we would all grab a big lunch and go to an amusement park, water slides, movies, or just all hang out together for deep conversations with our sales managers. I loved the sales contests. They were a lot of fun. If you would outsell your sales manager that week, you get to throw a pie in her face.

Throughout the summer, I met moms, dads, cabinet makers, a doctor, insurance salespeople, teachers, car repair people, farmers, and truckers while I was just 19 years old. I condensed meeting numerous folks from all levels of society into ten weeks, which was the key to forming my lifelong habits. You really can't say you know life if it was just you hanging out with one friend for the summer, or it was you hanging out with four of your friends for the summer, or you hanging out with a bunch of friends just drinking beer, or catching movies, or playing video games all summer. To me, this does not equate to developing any good habits or learning about life.

The Southwestern Company experience was life-changing because the habits taught in sales school caused me to overcome my fear of speaking to strangers. It forced me to repeat patterns regardless of good or bad results. They placed me in situations where I was required to internally motivate myself repeatedly in a noticeably short period of 10 weeks. In addition, all this took place while overcoming 100+ degrees of heat with 80% humidity. Amid all that, I was sweating, frustrated, and unappreciated, with dogs chasing me and people slamming their doors in my face. Yet, I continued to do what I had set my mind to while overcoming self-doubt and rejections every day. Wow, did I do all that? Yes, I did. And in fact, this led me to pay my way through USC without my father's support in my Junior and Senior year.

To succeed, working hard means doing the same thing repeatedly, regardless of whether you feel like it or not. If you can do it consistently for 21 days, then that habit is ingrained in you, and you can repeat the pattern repeatedly.

If you have never done anything so drastic, pick one task and do it for 20 minutes per day, repeat it daily, and in 21 days, you will have built a habit of doing it naturally.

i.e., waking up at 5:30 am, exercising 5 minutes per day, eating at 6 pm every night, walking around your neighborhood for 15 minutes after dinner, etc.

Recruiting – Against All Odds

I felt good in the fall when I returned to USC. I had done something that 99% of college students would not challenge themselves to do. I was happy with my summer results and started telling my roommates and friends about my experience and the money I made. Over and over again, I shared my experience; I asked my friends if they would consider joining me and working with me in the summer, and repeatedly, they said no. They rejected me.

Initially, I didn't care because I was still on cloud nine. Then I got better-recruiting scripts, and I practiced them. I handed out alumni testimonials, but nothing. I kept trying. Then I received interest from a few college students. Then after they spoke to their parents, they changed their minds. Geez, recruiting USC College students to sell books would be hard.

Then I received my plane ticket and confirmation that I had made it to the President's Club trip. It was to Mazatlán with air and hotel all paid. Wow, it was pretty cool. I had the opportunity to hang out with some of the top producers at the age of 20. Some kids made over $30K in the summer (that's $30K in 12 weeks in 1994), and a gal earned that from Cal Poly. Say what? I had to meet her.

Time and time again, I would walk up to people I didn't know and listen to what they had to say or take notes on their success secrets. Of course, I took a lot of notes. At my age, I was highly impressed with everyone. I also saw that they were no different than me. I realized I could achieve the same level of success if I continued to work hard, studied hard, and was teachable.

When I returned from the President Club trip, I asked a manager to come to USC to assist me with a recruiting presentation. Tom McCAuliffe came from Santa Barbara; we structured a summer work program interviews on campus. Twenty people showed up. About half the students checked the box they were interested in the program. Days later, about four signed a letter of commitment, but by the time we were ready to leave for Nashville, only two students had come with me.

After interviewing over 100 students and only bringing two students to sales school, I was disappointed. I wish I had better skills in recruiting. What did I say that I could improve? Why did they not feel confident this was something they could do? Was there more I could have said? Why aren't more people like me? Why was I turned on by this idea when most everyone was not?

Arriving at the sales school energized me once again. The training was excellent. The speaker was great.

Successful people choose to do what unsuccessful people are not willing to do, or successful people do all the things unsuccessful people decide not to do.

Mort Utley says these are the 5 Keys to Success:

1. Burning Desire
2. Fighting Spirit
3. Strive For Perfection
4. Perseverance
5. Faith in God

One of my recruits was Brad; the other was Rick. Then off we went. We were assigned to work in Burlington, North Carolina. My second summer was different; I drove instead of going door to door on my bicycle. And this time, my roommates had to find their bicycles. They worked in the city, going door to door. I drove through the countryside; it was fun. Some homes were far apart. That got to me sometimes, as it was harder to put three presentations together per hour and 30 presentations per day. When there was no one home or two homes in a row, you sometimes don't talk to anyone for an hour or two. I met many farmers. Gas was cheap back then, too; what a terrific way to see the United States.

Being a student manager was also different. I sold books in the daytime. Each night for 12 weeks, I had to ask my recruits about their day and how I could help them. I helped them with accounting and ordering books for delivery. But Brad had girlfriend problems at home, which distracted him from focusing during the workday. Does that sound familiar?

One day, Brad began missing his girlfriend, which evolved into missing his parents. Then it was a habit of not being able to get up in the morning, not doing well in sales, not interested in learning, and not interested in improving. Do you see the pattern? Next, I saw how one lousy habit developed into another bad one, and so on. Finally, after about six weeks of selling in the book field, he convinced me he would rather quit and go home.

I recalled when I didn't do well in Track & field and stayed with the team. Although I continued to work on my weak areas, I sought personal best improvement each week and at each competition. I didn't realize someone would quit without trying harder first. To me, building good habits was everything. Brad never played sports, as far as I remember. He never had any real work experience. Brad was very social but never spoke with any convictions in his voice.

Brad's failure was due to lacking a deep foundation of past successes or the ability to recognize sales cycles are all incremental patterns. Repeating each pattern regardless of how one feels like doing it or not and forming daily repeatable habits is just a numbers game towards success. Then having numerous past successes builds self-confidence, which establishes a foundation of a new faith that gives someone a higher purpose and reward. Rick was different. He was a good-looking guy, exceptionally smooth with a great smile, a ladies' man.

On our drive to Burlington, North Carolina, Rick was wise not to speed. A police car passed us at around 80 miles per hour, so we were good. But Rick decided to follow the police car at his speed. Then the police car chose to slow down to pull us over. How unlucky. Selling books was a new skill for Rick, but he adapted well. He was patient. Everything he did, he wanted to look cool doing it. His hair had to look perfect. He didn't like to sweat too much working in 100-degree heat. He wanted to do well for the summer but didn't express any big burning desire. Did he need to accomplish a particular financial goal? Was he willing to work hard, put in all the hours, study hard, memorize all the scripts, be teachable, and be service-minded?

It was exceedingly difficult to feed his ego or inspire him throughout the summer. Other student managers also chipped in to help, with no luck. Rick didn't make all his calls, as he didn't want to work too hard. At the end of the summer, he made some money for college, but not a lot. I would always wish people to do well and do what they said they would, and I was sad that Rick didn't do better than me. I always wished him well, regardless of the path he took after USC.

In my second year, I made the President's Club again. Again, the free trip to Mazatlán was great. Especially for a college student.

I agreed and decided to return, sell books the third summer, and bring some of my friends again.

In my Senior year at USC, I thought that with my sales and past recruiting skills, it would be much easier to recruit the second time around.

Work ethic-wise, the word got around because I had sold books; I had tenacity. As a result, the USC Student Government and the Student Senate recommended and approved me to be an appointed Officer. I would be the Elections Recruitment Chair with four units of tuition credit per semester.

In that position, I had to provide guidelines, instructions, do's and don'ts, cheating consequences, grievance committee, election day event planning, and vote counting for 32 student senators' positions at a budget of $1,000.

I got on the phone, and I called Coca-Cola, Del Taco, and various other vendors to see if they wanted to be event sponsors, and they did. So, I ended up pulling off one of the most significant elections for USC Senators at half the typical budget.

In my Senior year, I moved out of the Phi Kappa Tau Fraternity to live in an apartment with my industrial engineer roommate and two business major guys. After my classes and studies, I found myself naturally drawn to doing something else in my free time. I kept thinking about how many students I would recruit while doing my homework. That distracted me from my homework and learning.

In fact, as an Industrial Systems Engineer, I took all the easy courses in my first three years and stacked the most challenging courses in my Senior year. Classes like Civil Engineering, Mechanical Engineering, Thermal Dynamics, and electrical engineering courses were just required courses but did not pertain to my major. I didn't focus well and didn't care how well I did. I cared about recruiting; I wanted to succeed, and I wanted to be like all the top recruiters that were my same age. I had a shot.

To be the best, it's all about HABITS, HABITS, and HABITS... but Joe, you forgot to smile.

Like a scheduled class, I began to plan the hours I would work each day. I set goals for how many people I would need to approach each week. I broke it down to how many people I would need to reach out to per day to hit my goal. I measured my leads by who showed up at an interview, meeting a second time with those wanting training materials, and studying training materials. I began to see the same pattern again. Students don't show up for interviews; they don't show up for the follow-up; they don't want training materials; they don't want to study. Priorities were different for most college students. Getting real-world experience was not what they were focusing on at ages 20-21. People say one thing, and they do something else. I learned so much from selling books door to door, hearing from parents who don't want to buy books for kids, and now hearing it from college students; this helped me understand human nature more.

At the age of 21, without YouTube, social media, or google tips on working smart in recruiting, I continued to do what the school of hard knocks taught me. It was a numbers game. I read books and books on sales and recruiting. I used third parties selling, tied-downs, projections, testimonials, and the Benjamin Franklin close. I'd just kept at it. At the end of the summer, only two students came with me to Nashville Sales School. I was tremendously disappointed again, repeating 200% to 300% of the work but with the same results.

Graduation at USC was a blur. My parents and sisters came to see me. They saw that I'd received the distinguished Men of Troy Senior award given to only a handful of Seniors. My friend David from High School came also. He wanted to go to USC one time but never pursued it. Instead, he wanted to be an actor; he took some acting courses, then stopped. But I was glad to see him. Finally, I said goodbye to my friend Richard Doughty, with whom we shared many things in common at college. Several years later, he asked me to be the best man at his wedding.

Today Richard and I are both doing the same thing. We are both lenders providing home loans for folks. He's been at it for over 32 years, doing just one thing since college. I've done too many things to count since college. But unfortunately, David and Richard did not want to join me in selling books; they chose different paths.

Shortly after graduation, I got in my car with my recruits and another student manager, and we drove to Nashville. Arriving at Sales School, my Sales Manager, Fred Prevost, was super understanding. He spent time with me to ensure that I could disassociate my recruiting pain/disappointment to participate, engage and sell this summer. Fred even took me out of the sales meeting to have lunch with him. First, he ordered a salad; then, he took me to pick up his son from soccer. He realized I needed to de-stress and feel like a human instead of functioning and thinking like a machine. Unfortunately, I continued not knowing how to process failures except to keep doing more, focusing on the new results, and concentrating on future successes.

Surviving Being Off Schedule

One of my recruits decided to quit right after sales school. I don't even remember his name anymore as he left. Sometimes, we don't remember those who quit, right? Luckily, I still had one recruit with me, Greg. Another student manager named Peter, Greg, Stanley, and I were assigned to work at Ellicott City in Maryland. So off we went.

We arrived at Ellicott City and called many churches to see if they knew anyone who could rent a room to college students for the summer. No luck. We checked with past Alumni, but no luck. We used payphones to make many calls (no cell phones in 1986 yet, only pagers). We kept driving around, asking, then we came to a Korean-speaking family with an extra room to rent. How Greg knew how to speak Korean, I still don't remember, but hey, he got us a place to stay, and we were thankful.

Everything was going great. I didn't sell anything the first day, but everyone in the headquarters did. Everyone was excited. I was, too, as I knew that one zero-day would not make a lousy summer; the answer is always at the next appointment. I started slow, but I ended up with a good week, a little behind Greg and Peter.

During sales school and every week, Greg worked hard, studied hard, and was coachable. He was undoubtedly any student manager's perfect recruit

We all improved over the next few weeks. Then, at one of the Sunday meetings, we all met up after lunch to watch Top Gun. It was terrific; the movie was fantastic. Then, of course, we were all ninja salesmen, top gun salesmen, and all of us flying high in the following weeks.

On a Tuesday of one week, I was excited to meet some lovely families and kids. Afterward, I drove onto a gravel road to meet the next family. But I was going too fast around the turn, and when I braked, the back of the car spun out. The car drove itself straight into a creek next to the road. There was a big jolt as the vehicle jerked to a sudden stop by a big rock that prevented me from plunging down 20 feet into the creek. I was scared, screaming at the top of my lungs as the car lunged to a stop.

I got out of the car; the rain started drizzling down. I sat down on the gravel road as I was in total shock. Am I alive? Am I dead? I'm alive. Wow. What am I going to tell my brother? I totaled his car. How am I going to work? How am I going to get around? Was my summer over? It took about half an hour to see another vehicle coming through the turn to help me out. A truck with some chains, he pulled my car back up the road. He then towed my car to a garage. There, the owner confirmed there was nothing he could do to fix my car due to the frame damage.

My brother was not happy with me when he heard the news. My brother said why don't you fly home and help me run my auto business. He needed help. I turned him down, saying I came to Maryland to work this summer. I will stay because of my commitment. How would you like it if I came to work with you and quit a month after I started because I was in a car accident? My brother then left me alone, assisted with insurance claims, and I continued to figure out my life when everything was "off schedule."

I would say the scripted sales presentation daily compared to my first summer. Then, all I had to do was run between doors to be successful. The third summer, driving between homes, I had way too much time to think; the summer would have been better if I had worked in the city without any time to think and just kept knocking on doors one after another; that was the key I would remember.

Have you ever been off schedule? How soon did it take you to get back on Track?

Being 3,000 miles away from home, and without transportation, at age 22, I called my Sales Manager in Nashville. He said to buy a car and get back to work. So, I did it by faith.

I asked the folks at the garage if they had any cars for sale that would last me for the summer. The owner pointed to me a beat-up Toyota Corolla. I asked whether it would last me for three months. He said yes. I wondered how much. He said $400. I gave him $400, and we parted ways.

After that, I was not doing well selling the following week. So I called my sales manager. He said. "You need some inspiration and encouragement. Why don't you drive to Fredericksburg, Virginia, and work with superstar Dennis? You can work with him for a few days, remember how easy sales are, then you can get back on your own again."

Without questions, I drove to Fredericksburg, met with Dennis, followed him, and did what my manager Fred and Dennis said.

My recruit, Greg, was still doing a little better than me. As Greg had already established momentum, Fred and I decided to leave him selling in Maryland as I moved to Virginia. So we parted ways.

After following Dennis for a few days in Fredericksburg, I went back to knocking on doors. Sometimes, the odds were not in my favor. That led to taking longer break times. Then I would sit in front of a tree and repeatedly read Chapter Two of Og Mandino, The Greatest Salesman in the World. "I shall greet this day with love in my heart. I shall love the rain for it cleanses my soul; I shall love the sun for it warms my bones." OK, let's get to work. People said no, I didn't give in. But my mind was playing tricks on me; what was wrong with me? I called Fred. I was struggling.

I went back at night, and Dennis and Stewart were both doing very well, but I couldn't pull it together; how awkward, how embarrassing, and how frustrating. Self-doubt kept creeping in. Is this what I'm supposed to do for the rest of the summer? Why not just quit and go home? No one cares. No one will know. I kept reminding myself: that those who make it through the summers are the ones who think they can, or from Vince Lombardi's speeches when he said:

"Winning is not a sometime thing; it's an all-the-time thing. You don't win once in a while; you don't do things right once in a while; you do them right all the time. Winning is a habit, just like losing is a habit." Or when he said, *"I firmly believe that any man's finest hour, the greatest fulfillment of all that he holds dear, is when he has worked his heart out in a good cause and lies exhausted on the battlefield of battle - victorious. Wherever that battlefield might be"*

I kept reminding myself that however bad it got, I would finish the summer; I would not quit like my four years in Track & field. At this stage in my life, I would have packed up and gone home if it wasn't for the fact that my spiritual faith was deeply grounded. So instead, the rest of the summer includes working in the rain, in 100-plus degrees of heat, the radiator leaking, delivering books at the end of the summer in both Maryland and Virginia, and driving the clunker back to Nashville, Tennessee.

I didn't think I was a hero at all, but when I stepped foot at the Southwestern Company at the end of the summer, my sales manager Fred Prevost came up, greeted me, hugged me, and put his arms around my shoulder. He picked his shoulder up high, marched me into the building like a returned war hero, and told everyone how proud he was of me. While I didn't feel like I had a great summer, at least I didn't feel like I had a crappy summer anymore. I didn't quit when others did.

After checking out, I realized that instead of making the same amount as I had made in year two, I made only 50%. If I had quit early on, I would have gone home empty-handed. In fact, with that check, scholarships, loans, and tuition credit, I paid my way through USC through the Southwestern program. It was good enough. I was not a superstar in my mind, but I was not a quitter. So not being a quitter became my new pattern, my new habit. Always finish what you start, no matter what!

I drove home from Nashville with Stanley. I was to drop him off in Missouri before going home alone. About an hour from Stanley's house, near Columbia, my Corolla radiator started smoking, so I pulled over. I found some water, put it into the radiator, and started driving. Shortly after that, the engine locked up and died. Several hours later, I had the car towed to a garage for the second time in three months.

The owner then returned and said I had cracked the radiator, the car was totaled, and he couldn't fix it. Crap! On a brighter note, I spent $400 and drove a car for over 10,000 miles in eight weeks, which was a surprisingly good return on my $400 investment, right?

Stanley's parents came to pick us up. I then bought a plane ticket to fly home instead of driving. What a summer. How do I even explain all the events to anyone in my family or friends? Who has ever totaled two cars in three months?

During the three summers with Southwestern Company, I met and spoke with over 15,000 families and made over 5,000 sales presentations. The Southwestern Company has given me so much confidence in life, a positive attitude, and how to handle negativity and rejections in short three-month increments. I had developed more mental muscles than in any other jobs I knew. At the age of 22, this mental muscle was now part of me.

Today, many life coaches or sales coaches teach ideas without much substance or perspiration. Southwestern Company taught me three things:

1. Who to call (Pre-approaching)
2. Executing a repeatable habit every day for 21 days to 90 days (demonstration)
3. Follow up (answering objections). I learned it all for free without having to pay thousands of dollars, and I applied it and found financial success with it.

As Summer came to a close, a trip with all the salespeople to Puerto Vallarta was undoubtedly an enjoyable way to end my third-year affiliation with the Southwestern Company and move on with my life.

I also believe we need disappointments in our path to take a mental break and appreciate the callousness within which we have built. Then we are to make new choices on how to leapfrog upwards instead of reducing one's effort or quitting.

At this point, you can conclude that habits, habits, and habits drive success. That is the Game Changer. However, should you wish to stop reading further, I hope you and I are connected to know there is a solution with the time invested in reading so far. The answer is going from point A to point B daily to develop a pattern of the same activities and doing this pattern. Then refine and master your daily habits until you achieve success.

An example would be to spend 20 minutes per day reading this book. Then, over the next five days, based on the habit of reading this book, you would finish the book. Then read another book.

Where and how does one with this Habits Driven life skill test this learned theory?

Does applying good work habits and applying them to new opportunities work in everything for the next 35 years? Well, let's start from the beginning first.

Foundations of Faith

Chapter Two

Where do you learn how to build good habits?

What dominant memories do you have that you use to anchor the foundation of all your faith? What does that action look like when you believe in something, you take action?

Before I Was Born

My father, Wen Kho Siau, was a Baptist Minister for over 60 years, which meant he was doing the same thing over and over again for over 60 years, right?

If he were alive today, that would mean what he did during the last ten years would be the same as what my father would do today and what he would do in the next ten years, right?

At your employment today, if you know what you do today is the same thing that you will do ten years from now, and if you love it and continue to do it, you have faith.

If you do something else, then there's no faith and passion in what you're doing today, right? So what lens do you use to filter your pursuit today or ten years from now?

In the United States, it appears many people are always stuck with "I will only do what I love," "I haven't found my passion yet," or "I don't know my WHY, that's why I'm quitting, or doing something else," "or this is too hard, I rather do something easier than this." Whereas, in many Asian countries, with a thousand people always standing next to you wherever you are, we work each day regardless of whether we are passionate or feel like it. That's because if we don't say yes right away, thousands of people will do what we do for less in a society of a billion people. The Asian culture most often knows how to function under a survival *mindset*. The Eastern philosophy is why I work hard to stay alive and feed my family. There are no handouts. Whereas the Western philosophy is I need to find my purpose, or I'm not going to work that hard until I do. Or the government will always take care of me with 26 weeks to 52 weeks of unemployment pay.

My father lived in Taiwan; after high school, he served in the Taiwan army infantry for two years as a requirement as a citizen. Then he was ordained as a minister at the age of 25. My father and mother both left families with seven brothers and sisters. He married my mom when he was 26 and my mom was 22. And off they went.

Two years later, my oldest sister was born in Taiwan. My brother came two years later, and my second sister two years later. She was a 3.5 lb. baby, the smallest in our family.

One year later, while my mom was pregnant with me, a Malaysian church reached out to my father. There was a need and a calling, so my father accepted. So, my father brought my mom, two sisters, and brother to Malaysia. My father then continued his preaching in a Malaysian church. He did the same thing daily, giving a different message each Sunday and to a different crowd.

While my mom was in Malaysia, one day, she had labor pains. She went to the hospital, which was 3 hours away. When she arrived, the doctor said she was not ready to give birth yet. She returned to her home. Then the next day, she had labor pains again. She spent another 3 hours going back to the hospital; the doctor said she was not ready either, but my mom did not want to return home, yet the doctor had no beds. Somewhere along the way, they admitted my mom to the hospital, and I was born a healthy 8lb baby, the biggest of our bunch.

How My Mom Took Care of Us

Shortly after I was born, a Hong Kong Church reached out to my father. There was a need and a calling. Once again, my father accepted. Then my father brought my mom, my two sisters, my brother, and me to Hong Kong. My father continued preaching in a Hong Kong church for eight years.

Imagine my mom taking care of three kids in Malaysia, not knowing the language of the four of us, from an infant to age eight, living in Hong Kong. The only way to survive and buy groceries was to point to this or that for eight years, as the languages were different. My mom had studied to be a teacher, but it didn't work out well. So as a pastor's wife, she took care of us. That consumed most of her days.

I still remember growing up in Hong Kong. We had raised chickens for eggs in our bathrooms in our very tight condo in a tall brick building. One day, it was time to eat the chicken for dinner. My mom went into the bathroom and drained the chicken blood from the neck to make blood soup later. She then plucked the feathers off the chicken and cooked it for dinner. My mom was tough. She learned everything from her parents, who had struggled all their lives.

My mom's roots were in a city called Chia Yi in Taiwan. Her father worked for a bank. Her seven brothers and sisters were 18 years apart.

In Hong Kong, my oldest sister had gone to a bilingual school where they taught her one class of English per day. My brother and second sister all went to the same school as me.

Like the Joy Luck Club movie, we grew up with my parents never saying I love you. It wasn't until this movie came out that I realized the older generation, my grandparents, never said I love you to them. That's why they never learned or knew how to say I love you to us or me. Instead, my parents expressed love by repeating, "did you eat yet," "let's eat," "you need to eat more," "or let me put some food on your plate." To them, that's how they communicated love to us, through food or talk of food and feeding us. That's how their grandparents showed their love to them. They would say, "it's cold out there; make sure you take a jacket with you," "wear warmer clothes," and "don't forget to dress warmly." These endearments communicated was their way of saying, "I love you," to us as they had never heard those words before. They didn't know how to say it. Our parents provided for us. They provided a roof over our heads, food, and that's about it. That's all they knew.

I grew up not seeing my dad a lot. He was always absent.

Do you think you're unsuccessful because you lacked something from your parents?

How do your parents show their love?

My Father Immigrated to the US in 1972

Multiple churches continued to reach out to my father to preach in Taiwan, China, and Japan. So off he went. My poor mom! Since international phone calls were expensive, my dad would record a message to us on a cassette tape, mail it to us, and we would gather around and listen to dad talking to us and praying over us.

Then one day, a US church reached out to my father. There was a need and a calling. This time, my father would leave one year ahead of us. In 1972, he went to the US on a business visa. He arrived in the US with less than 10 US Dollars in his pocket. Just enough to buy food and make an emergency phone call if no one picked him up at the airport right away. Upon arrival, he slept at the church office. They offered him a $2,000 monthly salary to start, but he had to buy a car, which cost him $2,000.

A church member then co-signed for my father to purchase a 1,100-square-foot home a year later for $24,000 (if we had only kept the house today). Finally, in August 1973, our family immigrated to the US, and we hugged dad at the airport on arrival.

In short, my father's foundation was faith. His anchor was in religion. My father's strong faith in God caused him to take action repeatedly, without the ifs and's or buts. Let's pick up and move. Let's pick up and move again. Let's move again, like a military family. None of us knew what awaited us, or the challenges ahead for mom, for us, for not knowing English, not knowing the culture or the laws, or not having any friends.

Through daily actions and repetitive trial and error, an opaque future slowly unfolded in front of us with each new journey. My brother, sisters, and I didn't speak English. We were teased and made fun of because of our funny haircuts and out-of-style clothes because our pants were too short (which is a fresh style today). I got into fights whenever they made fun of me and bullied me. We all wore donated hand-me-downs from other siblings. We ate at churches and at friends' homes to save money. The patterns were the same. We did the same thing every day and the same thing every Sunday.

One common theme throughout our family was that we had developed a tremendous amount of FAITH. Our outcome was that we would always be OK (based on our faith in religion). We know that every action we take is blessed regardless of the adversities that come our way. Thank you, dad, that 50 years ago, your calling was to go to the US alone, with nothing, and to prepare a home for us and to immigrate here in 1973. #PricelessJourneys

If neither you nor I have good parenting, where do we go from here?

Growing Up in the US

At age 10, I saw something incredible. I saw my 14-year-old brother getting up at 5:00 am on Saturdays and Sundays to deliver newspapers. First, he made money by delivering papers every day. Then he doubled his paper route. Next, he used his money to buy a better, cooler bicycle, followed by a car. Then he fixed a car, made money, and did it again with another vehicle.

Habit Forming Journeys and Failures

Delivering Newspapers

I saw a pattern of success that I replicated with similar faith and actions. First, I got up early. Then, I folded the newspaper the same way for two years, doing the same thing every day. I delivered newspapers. Because of the money rewarded, I bought a bicycle and bought another bike like my brother.

Playing Piano

My sisters played the piano; I played the piano for six years. I played for 20 minutes to one hour daily, doing the same thing every day as they did.

Running Track and Field

My brother ran Track for four years. I saw a new pattern. With similar faith and similar actions, one would expect I would have the same success. But no, I didn't have the same results. I ran, hurdled, and ran the one mile, but I didn't have the same success. After four years, I realized I was not physically created like my brother. I would not be the one who could race and win every time with a 1st, 2nd, or 3rd prize reward. I sucked! Maybe it would be best if I just blended in with the team. Excelling in sports was not a high point for me, but I stayed in Track and Field all four years without winning anything, but I didn't quit.

Playing the Trumpet

I started playing the trumpet in seventh grade. That was under my initiative without seeing my sisters, brother, or anyone else in my family doing it first. Like playing piano with a piano teacher, I got a trumpet coach. Then when I went into High School, I was a badass trumpet player. Then my ego set in; I tossed aside my coach and played in the marching band, jazz band, and orchestra. I was great at playing the Trumpet; I was cool. I received endorphins that I did not get from anything else. I continued. I practiced and became better. I had jam sessions with other players, and I got better.

With endorphins, I felt great. Knowing I was good at something no one else was, I continued playing for the Santa Clara Drum and Bugle Corp. I learned a unique style of precision playing for competition as I traveled across the United States with 80 other guys and gals.

We were on the road with an 8 am wake-up call every morning. Then after cold showers, practice started every morning at 9 am. Then lunch, more rehearsals, back on the road, competitions, sleeping on high school gym floors, and we would do it all over again for 30 days. I was forming habits, calluses on my hands, and my lips embouchure strengthened. Like with bigger muscles, I could play longer and louder with four hours of playing daily.

After one summer of this, I turned in my Santa Clara Vanguard feather. It was too much for me; I learned there were limitations again. Playing in High School marching bands was much more fun than practicing and building good habits in 100 degrees of heat traveling across the country. Deep down, I knew many players there were naturally better than me. I learned that it was a poor tradeoff for my endorphins and competition, and I finally gave up after finishing what I started after one full year.

I wanted this feeling so bad and for this feeling to continue. The summer before college, I even became a summer camp music instructor, but that didn't do it for me either, as my roommate was a better trumpet player and teacher than me. My high highs had peaked.

I played for the USC Trojans Marching Band for my first year in college. While they were the craziest bunch of folks, much better players than me, many things happened behind the scenes. The four hours of rehearsals per day twice a week to performing eight hours on game day was a poor tradeoff for me. I gave up again and didn't return to the USC Trojans Marching Band for my second year, but I finished what I started for one full year as I did with the Santa Clara Vanguard.

I had years of playing, built great playing habits, became overconfident, did not want to practice, and couldn't see the tradeoff rewards of playing, so I gave up.

Am I just like you? Are we more similar than different?

Moving

In my high school days, before my sophomore year, my dad received another call, so we moved to Cupertino, CA, where he started working for a church in Mountain View, CA.

At one church camp I attended, I remember what one speaker had said. Though not directed at me, I took it upon faith, which has continued to change my worldview.

Reading the Bible

The pastor said if you spend 20 minutes reading the Bible every day, you can finish reading the Bible in one year. So I did that in my sophomore year. After school, before my friends called me to ride our bikes and hang out at the park, I would sit down on the Recaro car seats my brother put in my room; I would spend 20 minutes reading the Bible, and guess what? I read the whole Bible in 1 year!

I was proud of myself for this accomplishment. I was proud of myself as not many 16-year-olds had read the Bible from cover to cover. I was proud that I knew the bible stories better. As a result, I became better anchored in my faith and my foundation of belief. After that, I had higher self-esteem and faith since I could do something not many people have done. Daily reading of the Bible carried me in many unique ways for the rest of my life.

1. By learning how to break down an enormous, cumbersome task, such as reading a whole bible, into increments of 20 minutes of daily reading, I could take on larger projects and work on them in smaller bites size increments to get the job done.

2. I believed the bible stories; I believed in God - which takes faith. It takes faith to believe in something you cannot see and touch. I believe that. This kind of faith then translated to whatever was difficult for me in the future. By assuming and believing it would work out for me, I would have peace going through difficult times. I don't have to worry. I need to remember that God has been faithful, and I should be faithful and not give up. Every day, I rest assured that God has been watching over my steps.

I stayed with my father for two years in Cupertino. Then he got another call and accepted his calling again. This time he went to Brazil for two years during my Senior year in High School and my first year in college. Unfortunately, my father did not attend my high school graduation.

From your earliest childhood memories, what repetitive tasks and habits can you journal that have defined your willingness to take upon daily tasks, projects, or work longer than one year, two years, or three years? Why did you continue, or what were your reasons for quitting?

On a scale of 1 to 10, where do you put your faith in religion as an anchor for your success?

Adoption of All Ideas Entrepreneur

Chapter 3

Where do you learn how to build good habits?

After graduating from USC, most college students would immediately find a job, work, and repay their student loans. I was a maverick. Besides recruiting college students and driving 3,000 miles across the country to sell books door to door, I got on a plane a month later when I returned home in August. I went on a three-month international trip to Taiwan, Hong Kong, China, Thailand, Malaysia, and Singapore. I visited many cities I didn't remember from 13 years ago. I met many of my relatives and my brother's clients there and went sightseeing all over Asia.

Like selling books, I purposefully put myself into an environment where I could meet many people in a noticeably short 90 days. However, deliberately positioning myself in a contrary environment has been my model in forcing myself to adapt to changes quickly.

"We are always so much more than the bad things that happen to us. Sometimes you just need to learn that you can't wait until life isn't hard before you decide to be happy." – Nightbirde from AGT

Travel to Taiwan

While in Taiwan, I took a 2-hour Chinese class every day for six weeks. I attended numerous trade shows, including meeting a manufacturer with an incredible product design. He owned the patent and design for a one-hand automatic closing umbrella. I proposed to sell his product in the US. He agreed that I would be his salesperson in the US. I had no idea how to penetrate the US Market. I had no clue how shipping/receiving, letters of credit, US marketing/sales, or payment collections worked. But I was driven. I was a go-getter, just like with the Southwestern Company.

Sell Umbrellas, Automotive, Lehman Brothers, Network Marketing Umbrellas

After I returned to the US, I knew that in everything, sales come first, then you can figure out the rest later. So I took this unique idea, added my habits, executed the seven selling cycles, and took it to market. The sales cycle involves pre-approaching, approaching, establishing rapport, introducing, demonstrating, answering objections, and collecting cash.

One day, I learned about an entrepreneurial conference in February 1987 in Chicago. My brother gave me some money and booked me a flight and hotel. Michael Dell of Dell Computer was a speaker at the conference. He was recognized as the entrepreneur of the year; how cool was that?

During one of the convention breaks, it was snowing and freezing cold outside. But it was still crucial for me to push my product to retailers. So, I decided to do what I did when selling books door to door. I walked up and down Michigan Avenue in the snow. I walked into Marshall Fields and other department stores. Then, without knowing anyone, I'd just ask to see the managers and the department store buyers.

When a manager came out, I established rapport, gave a quick self-intro, and demonstrated how the one-handed closing umbrella worked; I left them a sample and some flyers, exchanged phone numbers, and said I would call them back in a few days.

A week after I had returned, Hammacher Schlemmer, one of the larger high-end mail-order outfits, called me, and they gave me an order for 500 units, then another 1,500 units, another 3,000 units, dang, I was in the big league, I thought. Then, of course, challenges hit. Five hundred units, no problem; I used my cash. I sent the manufacturer the 20% upfront deposit, and I received payment from Hammacher Schlemmer 60 days after they received their order. So the velocity of my money was recycled every 90 days; it was incredible—done. I made a 50% gross profit margin, which was not bad.

When the order size got more substantial, I realized I didn't have adequate funds for a 20% deposit for the manufacturer to buy parts and start production. Then a 5,000-unit order came; it was a Christmas order. So my brother and I got a bank to issue me a letter of credit with an IOU to pay. Then November, the shipment did not come; Thanksgiving came and went, and the shipment had still not arrived. The manufacturer kept saying parts were unavailable. The spring for the umbrella was unavailable. As December's first and second weeks came and went, the shipment still had not arrived. The one-hand closing umbrellas shipment had still not arrived by Christmas or January.

February came, and Hammacher Schlemmer canceled their order with me based on non-delivery. Then in April, my entire order arrived. The manufacturer would not cancel their produced order based on the agreed contract. As a result, my brother's garage was stocked with over 5,000 units of umbrellas, and I still owed 80%. I had no other buyers. It was a terrible experience to start a business. I tell you, it took over 30 plus years to get rid of these umbrellas through Christmas gifts, white elephant gifts, birthday gifts, and personal use, and I still have some umbrellas in every corner of my house today. Then I still had to swap out past damaged inventory with warranty replacement. The sales, production of funds for the deposit, the upside, and the downside, taught me all about the hard knocks of retail. The memories of what it takes to run an importing/exporting business were priceless when I earned $0 net at the end of the day.

Could I have repeated this process, found another product overseas, requested an exclusive, brought it to the market, and pitched it to Walmart, Macy, Safeway, Amazon, BestBuy, Dicks, Bath Beyond, etc.? Sure, I could have. But the retail game never made sense to me after my first exposure. What if I have a three-million-dollar order? What if the shipment was on a container ship, items were not received in the warehouse by a specific date, and retailers canceled the order? How am I going to sell or discount the inventory without going bankrupt?

It was an early lesson that saved me many times over. Some unique products can look flashy and attractive in the retail merchandising world, but it comes with a lot of financial inventory balancing unless the Shark Tank is behind you, right? And we have not discussed piracy yet.

Automotive Sales

In exchange for the car I had totaled from my brother and the trip to Chicago, and all the financial balancing we had to do, I worked for my brother in his automotive shop free for about six months. It was a family business. My brother ran an auto body restoration shop for European Autos. He would take a Porsche 911, cut down the front wheel nose fenders where the headlights pop up, and convert it to an aftermarket Porsche 930 with a slanted nose. He does terrific work with his paint booth. Other auto body shops could not match his quality due to his specialization in this unique area.

In a market with so many auto body repair shops, I saw firsthand the distinct competitive advantage one has by specializing in a niche market. Backed by the company name that matched the niche, Conversion Techniques was a well-known brand in the Bay Area in the early 90s.

Lehman Brothers

While working with my brother, with the umbrella ventures going on, one of my passions was to become a Stockbroker. So, I started calling all the brokerage firms to see if there were available positions and how to apply. This phase was before the internet age in 1987. Nothing was online, which meant I looked in the phone book. I looked up and called the phone number in the phone book one by one. Then, in May

1987, I landed a position and started working as a cold caller at Lehman Brothers. My brother let me pursue this to start making money on my own, but I returned three months later as he needed me again. While at Lehman Brothers, a stockbroker told me I should call and meet with Phil Parham. He had sold books door to door while attending Yale. After we connected, my life took another turn.

Phil told me he didn't trust the guys on Wall Street and there was something better he was doing. So, we met. Phil asked me to investigate network marketing as a vehicle to establish my financial freedom. I was intrigued by the concept at the age of 23. I had nothing to lose.

Network Marketing

Phil and his mentor, Steve, said that five years from today, you will be the same person you are today except for the people you associate with, the tapes you listen to, and the books you read. So I began reading more books, listening to more tapes, and hanging around with folks above my ambition level.

I learned from Steve that when your dreams and goals are more significant than the fears and obstacles in your way, then you will overcome your fears and obstacles and accomplish what you set out to do. That stuck with me to this day. It's all about your WHY. Why do you do what you do? What's your I-Beam, he called it? Or what's your hunger drive or your prey drive? What's your burning desire?

Five years from now, will what you do today give you financial freedom? If not, what's going to change? It certainly was not a guarantee working at Lehman Brothers as a cold caller. So I agreed with Phil and began recruiting a downline in network marketing.

I started by asking my best friend David, who went to my USC graduation, if I could get his opinion on a business venture. He and I sat down with Phil, and it made sense to Dave, so off we went; we signed up and committed to a new partnership.

One day, I took a carpool to go to San Francisco. I met a CPA. I asked him, five years from now, doing what you do today, will you have financial freedom? He said no. I asked him to check out a business tape and chat afterward. He did. He joined my network.

On and on I went. Like selling books door to door, I had high expectations in recruiting. I spoke to everyone within three feet of me—belly to belly. My insurance agent joined my network. Property managers, realtors, and dentists all joined my network. Some said yes, and some said no. Then I pull the group together to do coaching, product use training, and how-to recruit training. I called my friends and met them at their homes or Denny's. I prospected strangers at Safeway; as I waited in lines at various retail stores, my parent's friends, and just about anybody. I picked them up, drove them to meetings, and allowed them to meet more successful people.

I believed in the vision of being financially independent by 30, and I was willing to work for it. So, I worked hard and fast. After 90 days, I realized that my downline did not work as I did. None of them worked as hard and as fast as I was working.

Like with Southwestern recruiting, I kept my head down and continued to recruit. Ten people signed up and paid $100 for the starter kit, 20 people, 30 people, 40 people, and 50 people; I still didn't find anyone with my desires, drive, or appetite for success.

I was so gung-ho. There was a period I didn't watch TV for a year. And I had developed a mantra script that I would say every day before I made calls or talked to people.

Then an opportunity opened to expand our network marketing business into Mexico. I remember meeting several Mexicans from the Chicago Entrepreneurs Convention. So I called them and asked them if they would be interested in starting a franchise business with me in Mexico, and they said yes. Then I started planning to meet them in Mexico.

One year later, the details and process were set up and ready. Then, in 1990, I went to Guadalajara on my own. I booked a hotel and asked folks to come to the hotel to meet me every hour. And they did. Then I went back a second time to Mexico City. Then my engineering friend, my downline, and I went to Tijuana on my third trip.

There was so much excitement and disappointment I had experienced with Network Marketing. I had recruited 60 people in the US in three years; I had recruited over 60 people in Mexico in three months. I had spent a massive amount of my time, money, and effort, but the return was not there. Frustrations compounded. Like in the book field, I had called Phil multiple times to figure things out.

Why are folks not as motivated as me? Why do people say one thing and do something else? Why are adults not accountable? Why do people say they have dreams and goals and don't take action?

Patterns started to repeat themselves. Whether they were college students or adults, a small percentage of folks have developed a solid foundation of faith. But unfortunately, some have not developed long-lasting habits, confidence, or willingness to pursue their desires.

I learned from the Southwestern Company training to find college students with a burning desire.

At one junction, I was a property manager. I asked the prospective tenant, are you happy being a doctor, or are you open to other businesses to generate income? He said sure; he was open to the idea. I explained to him about network marketing. He was interested. After he joined, his sister joined, and their business grew faster than mine. I was happy. Finally, it was such a joy that someone caught a glimpse of a better future, and I was instrumental in their success.

All the while, I worked for my brother initially for free for the first six months, then three months at Lehman Brothers. After that, I went back to work for my brother again as he promised to pay me $1,000 per month—not much to brag about after graduating from USC. Finally, in May 1989, three years after graduating from USC, I was done working for my brother or family business. I was offered employment at the Department of Defense as an Industrial Engineer. Then I reduced my time to just helping my brother on Saturdays only. As a civilian working for the US Government, I was glad

I now had medical and 401K benefits instead of not having these benefits in a family business.

First Engineering Job

Being an engineer for the Department of Defense was pretty cool. They handed me a twenty-million-dollar project to manage on day one. It was from the construction to a functional aircraft painting facility for P3 Orion's, A6 Intruders, S3, and the F15s. Once the facility was turned on and operational, I had to coordinate from an engineering mindset, getting the right facility crew to resolve all environmental waste treatment plant challenges, air quality permitting, filtrations, and all operational challenges. I was always the onsite property manager, managing more than half a dozen to a dozen facility improvement projects.

With my background, I then submitted a beneficial suggestion as there were several hundred commercial air filters in the three hangars that they used to capture paint particulates during aircraft re-painting. They needed to be changed every three months or four times per year. I calculated if the filters were just as efficient after four months and were changed every four months or three times per year instead, that would save the US Taxpayers over $200K plus per year in material costs. The beneficial suggestions were approved. With that, I believed I had served our country well, with Joe being a #ProblemsSolvingPro.

Because there were so many delays and unproductive time working in the public sector, it was perfect for me to continue purging the umbrellas, work on my network marketing business at night, and help my brother on the weekends.

My manager, Harold Brown, would tease me and say, "Joe, you went to USC; you should be in the big time. You shouldn't be working in the government; you should run the world. So, what's an SC grad doing here?"

Continental Singers, Movie Extras, Legend Media, UARCO

Continental Singers

Then like my father, an opportunity surfaced; there was a calling, and I accepted. I was to perform with the Continental Singers in June 1992. I was so interested in playing my Trumpet as my last hurrah at age 28 at the 1992 Barcelona Olympics while traveling around the world performing church music and doing my ministry.

I then had to begin to raise $2,000 for the missionary trip. I asked my friends to sponsor my trip because of my faith and what I wanted to accomplish. I send out sponsorship letters and partnership letters. I gave a presentation of my faith, and I called folks. Then I quit my job after three years at the Department of Defense. I was ready for wherever God would lead me. Instead of Barcelona Olympics, I was re-assigned to do two months of ministry in the US, then fly to Sweden and perform in Poland, Estonia, Latvia, and Lithuania.

It was a one-month habit of performing with the Santa Clara Drum and Bugle Corp. It was a three-month habit of selling books in the summertime three years in a row. It would be a three-month habit of traveling through the US and Overseas performing with the Continental Singers. The same thing. Brush, rinse, and repeat.

We practiced in Denver and met other performers from all parts of the United States and the world. Then, each morning, we would pack our tour bus and go to the next city to perform at churches. I played the trumpet while others sang and gave bible messages. We then invited folks to join the church. We had host families who took us into their homes, where we spent the night. After that, we drove across the farm states, Iowa, North Dakota, Minnesota, Chicago, Pennsylvania, and Massachusetts, to New York, where we flew to Sweden.

Our band consisted of kids from 18 to 28. I was the oldest at the time. Some of us got along; sometimes, there was drama as we all came from different backgrounds. We were not always on time; we made fun of bad situations, and some were homesick and missing boyfriends or girlfriends, just like on the book field.

Instead of totaling two of my cars in the book field, the bus driver had two tires blow out at one time. While we were in Chicago, my trumpet valves were jammed. I was approved to go rogue and take a taxi through Chicago to get my trumpet repaired. It was a fun detour.

Poland was a very gray city with gray skies and buildings. To add to that, people wore gray. So, it felt like a lifeless city.

Estonia, the country, just became an independent state of Russia. Some people there have that old, rugged, wrinkled smile on their faces. There were many older generations of seniors, not too many young adults or teenagers, and a significant age gap everywhere.

Lithuania appears relatively poor. I saw seniors waiting in a bread line two blocks long for bread distribution from the bakery/government.

In Latvia, I stayed with a host family. At dinner, all she had to feed me was a couple of small pieces of rye bread with cucumber and tomatoes like tapas, and that was it. I woke up utterly starving the following day but was very appreciative she had fed me the best she had. That was all she had, and she gave it all to me. I knew she was a good person and would receive many blessings in her lifetime.

Every night for about three weeks overseas, we performed in English with a Russian translator. We drew tens and hundreds of people as they wanted to see the liveliness of Americans. They all have a dream of a better life.

Upon returning, we returned to Denver for a joint concert with like 15 other missionary groups of Continental Singers. It was over 500 of us performing with Sandy Patty, Michael W Smith, and Wayne Watson. It was very cool. The following clip showed our final 25th Anniversary performance: I'm in this two-hour video at 7:39 and several additional clips. https://www.youtube.com/watch?v=SekvE3w0Pic

After the concert was over, I called my parents. They told me that my manager Byron Dong at the Department of Defense, wanted me to return to work with them again. However, I had to decide quickly as the government position would close soon. So, when I returned, I helped my brother for about a month, accepted the position, and went back to work for the government again.

In the following years, my brother gave me two BMWs to drive, but I blew the two BMW engines one after another. Can you believe it? What luck I have with cars. One was an engine gasket that leaked; the other was compression failure. I'm not perfect.

Movie Extras

For fun, I was cast as a movie extra in a Robin Williams movie, "What Dreams May Come," and a movie extra as an SF Police Officer driving a police car across the Bay Bridge twice. I also made many friends resulting from being an escort at the Miss Chinatown and Miss Asian American Pageant for two years.

Legend Media

Then one day, my friends asked me to be the PR manager for their movie startup business. While I had no skills in the Television or the Movie industry, I knew about prospecting and talking to people. So, I accepted the Public Relations role with this business startup. Yes. I started engaging Asian movie actors, CEOs, and Politicians to see if they wanted to be interviewed by our company as we were trying to launch a pilot TV show focusing on Asian American successes. Unfortunately, several months later, after producing our first feature, the CEO did not raise additional funding. She decided she wanted to cut her financial loss, so we all disbanded the startup and went our separate ways.

Ultimate Aircraft Refinishing Company (UARCO)

Then another day, another opportunity presented itself. As the government was doing naval base closure, the Naval Air Station was shutting down. The production manager of the same $20 million painting facility wrote a business plan to privatize the government painting facility for local business redevelopment use. He named me the Director of Engineering and to be part of his business startup management team. I accepted.

Then off we went; I oversaw negotiating the lease of 120,000 square feet of aircraft corrosion control and aircraft painting facility. We agreed that the rent was $1 for the first year due to the tremendous startup cost and facility improvement requirement. We were in contract to paint the Chilean Government P3 Orion's.

The CEO was to get an SBA loan and a 100% matching grant. He then would be eligible for an additional line of credit. But for some reason, he was at retirement age and had second thoughts. After four months of negotiating with the government, he canceled the project right before accepting the final terms of the lease. It was not the risk or a worthwhile investment he wanted to take on for his family at his age.

After my return, I worked for the Department of Defense for another three years and finished as a GS 12 Engineer when the base shut down.

UC Berkeley Continuing Education, Tax License, Real Estate & Loan Broker, IBM

UC Berkeley Continuing Education

We were offered retraining benefits as part of the committed engineering team that agreed to remain as the shutdown crew for the Alameda Naval Air Station base closure. As a result, I received the opportunity to pick up two Certification Programs at UC Berkeley. 16-semester units each. One was Advanced Environmental Law, and the other was Business Management, Business Negotiation, and Marketing, where I received A+ in both curricula due to my worldwide insights.

In the marketing class, I spearheaded and proposed launching a new Nokia phone with a flipped keyboard two years ahead of its time. Like my umbrella import, I established how to break into the US Market, different marketing channels and distribution tiers, eliminated entry barriers, reduced costs, and created sales incentives to scale production yearly. At age 31, taking 32-semester unit courses and finishing them in nine months while working and running several side businesses could have been hard for some folks. Still, it was all about discipline and following the proper habits to meet the desired results and deadlines. I was so thankful when I completed all the courses.

Tax License

Furthermore, on my own, I studied and passed the CA State Tax license and CA Notary license and prepared taxes and notaries for folks.

Real Estate & Loan Broker

I also took and passed the real estate broker license and the 120 hours of Graduate Realtor Institute, GRI designation to help folks buy and sell real estate and do loans.

Just like in Southwestern Company, if you want immediate success, do a lot of activities in a brief period; this is how you receive more results in a shorter time and close more transactions vs. waiting for folks.

Being trained to do loans was not very interesting in the beginning. I didn't see how the whole operation worked. Nothing clicked with me, as nothing was repetitive.

Then I moved on to buying a foreclosure home at the court steps in Oakland. I pulled out the carpet, painted, hired folks to take things to the dump, and put in new kitchens and bathrooms. Unfortunately, I must have bought the home in the wrong area of Richmond. There was a gunshot hole in the windows the next day I went by the property.

On another property, after fixing it and installing a new carpet, and getting it listed on the market, a squatter broke in, dirtied the carpet, and stayed there for days. In another property, there was a significant amount of termite problems, and the foundation needed bolting. But the one that broke the straw on the camel's back was a home I had listed on Oakland Hill. Unfortunately, it burned down over a Thanksgiving weekend. Then the Seller asked me to locate a contractor to help her to rebuild, and I did.

After rebuilding the home, the Seller asked me to re-list it. When I walked into the house, the flooring was slanted. The contractor didn't build the home on a solid foundation, ugh.

Then the Seller asked me to help her short-sell her home in 1997. I called that a sign from God. When a house listed for sale burned down, it was time to get out of the business, and I did.

IBM

One day, another call came in, and a contracting company asked if I wanted to start working at IBM next week as a Facilities Engineer to get their M Class Clean Room constructed and put it online for production; I said yes. So, I rented a room from my friend, moved to Milpitas in two days, and started working at IBM the following Monday.

I was at IBM for less than six weeks when I received an offer from another job by a contracting company. The proposal was to start working at Hewlett-Packard in 10 days. That was 1998. I gave my resignation to my contracting company and IBM and proceeded to rent a place and move to Roseville on my own.

Moving to Roseville, CA – Hewlett Packard

Moving to Roseville

Moving to Roseville was great. I was so fortunate I didn't need to be stuck in the Silicon Valley traffic every day. The Bay Area commute was horrible. I got situated and found the best way to get to work. With my salary increase instead of low to no income for the prior three years just educating myself at UC Berkeley, real estate, loans, taxes, and business startups, this was an excellent payback.

Twelve years since graduation, world travels, overseas relationships, network marketing failure, and agonizing over mental and emotional disappointment were all priceless. As a result, I developed new business approaches, patterns, and life skills.

Hewlett Packard

Starting at Hewlett-Packard was a healing process, from having a clean slate to moving forward. I could finally focus on just one thing and turn to a new chapter in my life. Can you guess how long I stayed with Hewlett-Packard? Three years.

And within five months of my transition, I closed on purchasing my first home at $242K at 95 dollars per square foot with a 7.125% interest rate, paying 1 point.

Would you or would you let your children pursue something for three years without generating much income? Why?

Going back to Engineering was not that hard as I had many ideas to contribute, with real-world experience and excellent people skills. Industrial Engineers focus on being the project manager of the project. We communicate amongst all parties so Product Engineers and Marketing can speak and understand each other while managing vendors, test engineers' results, project timelines, and due. We are the efficiency expert in finding ways to shorten deadlines, reduce expenses, and increase profit. On day one, they assigned me to support HP T Class Servers, then the New Product Introduction that was rolling out with the V Class Servers and the Superdome, and coordinate a Production Line move from multiple buildings to the new one-site factory.

Application of ideas is based on what you learned, recalled, and can apply. Right?

Lots of work, lots of people, and lots of meetings to the point that we all joke about why we don't do what Intel does. Put up a clock and a dollar meter on the wall. When each person walks into a twenty-people meeting, everyone enters their employee number into a gadget, and the algorithm will display how much each production meeting costs the company.

Then several months after I started, my friend, the late Garrett Mock, asked me to go to China with him. Garret was a high-end realtor from Mountain View Coldwell Banker. When I started as a realtor, I called several realtors to establish referral relationships. He would call me every few weeks to say hello, and we became excellent friends.

Garret was getting married to his fiancé Lily. He wanted me to be his best man. Also, because Garret is Chinese but doesn't speak Chinese, he wanted my assistance translating Chinese for his wife's family. I agreed.

Growing up, my parents spoke Taiwanese to me. I started first grade in Hong Kong, so I spoke Cantonese primarily to my parents. I learned Mandarin from my classes in Taiwan, listened to music, and followed the written words while watching Chinese action movies with subtitles. That's how I could speak with Lily's parents, my wife, and to about 25% of all my clients today who are Asian.

This trip to China was also a life-changing event for me; I met my wife.

1. My father was a minister and immigrated our family to the US
2. Working for the Southwestern Company
3. Moving to Roseville
4. I met my wife in China

What were three events that were life-changing for you? How did you handle it?

Many of my friends wondered how I met my wife, Marina or if we had met on the internet. No, Marina was the hotel manager where Garrett's wedding event occurred. Just like the South Pacific song. Some enchanted evening, across the crowded room, you will see a stranger, and somehow you know.

While I was the hotel guest, I made many attempts to speak with Marina, but she was always busy attending to all the guests or work activities.

Marina was born in China and consistently employed by 4 or 5-star hotels as a local expatriate working for Chinese hotel chains. In other words, she would get paid the equivalent of a US Salary, about six times what local Chinese workers typically receive. Her role was whenever a hotel was about to finish construction, the hotel would fly her into the cities three months in advance. She has three months to set up Front Desk Policy Procedures and hire and train staff from housekeeping to Restaurant, Banquet to Food and Beverage. Once everyone knows their role, then they roll out the grand opening. That was her job. She was launching hotels to hotels through China for Crown Plaza and Holiday Inn mainly.

When I returned to the US several days later, I left a message for Marina, and she called me back. That was when prepaid calling cards were $0.60 per minute. Then many stories in our lives continued after that.

Hewlett-Packard was going through a lot of changes at the time. Carlie Fiorina came and spoke at Roseville. Her ideas for problem-solving were unique. She set a higher bar for me. Instead of justifying option one or two, she challenged us to shoot for accompanying the two options together as a solution even when the two solutions are quite the opposite. Instead of building a product based on profit or quality alone, build a quality product that makes a high profit.

When my two years contract at HP came to an end, I had to decide. I could quit being a contractor for at least one day, then see if I could secure a new HP contract to come back for another two years or take the full-time HP Salaried position they offered. However, I would need to take a 50% salary reduction. So, I took the role of an HP Employee and started a new role as a project manager for the Japanese OEM Group. Instead of being a nobody for a day, I was now a corporate employee with corporate benefits instead of no benefits as a contractor.

In the Japanese OEM Group, whenever a server or server component fails in Japan, our group was to provide a root cause analysis response with the reasons for component failure. We would deliver a written report and make a presentation to Japanese senior management in Japan. Between the quarterly face-to-face meetings, we had weekly meetings to add or subtract from the component failure list. These meetings went on and on each week. We flew to

Japan and met our customers face to face. They flew to the US too. It was a very engaging corporate ritual, an almost ceremonial experience each time.

Then In January 2001, when the tech bubble burst, many companies started to report layoffs, as in 1987 and 1995. Hewlett-Packard was also going through a workforce reduction process. So, since I had less than one year of tenure in April 2001, my employment ended.

Just like being laid off from the Department of Defense, I knew many good things would come from this again. With my foundation of faith, I knew that everything would work out. That was just a year and a half after being married.

After being exposed to 14 various employment industries in 15 years, I wondered what I should pursue permanently. Engineering jobs were drying up in Silicon Valley too. So, with my engineering mind and being good with numbers, I chose to do something with numbers.

I thought the only thing that made sense was to work in the banking world. Through my Asian travel, I saw how annually, with a 5% population growth, thousands to millions of folks constantly need checking, savings accounts, car loans, home loans, and banking services. Doing home loans with my math and sales background made sense, as loans are repetitive skills. I would be able to master them because good habits are built based on developing the same daily routines. However, I was not going to do real estate full time, too much driving, and not an easy way to establish the same daily routine every day.

Bending to Different Cultural Ideas

Chapter 4

What do you mean you don't get it?

When you were young and went to college, didn't most people around you think differently than you did and disagree with you? But, on the other hand, didn't that open up your capacity to entertain, learn and adapt to new ideas? Since then, if you have formed good habits in your personal life and your ways of daily living are set, how likely are you able to adapt to foreign ideas constantly?

Marriage, Annual Vacations, Raising Kids

If people are from two different continents, do they think the same? For example, are Men from Mars and Women from Venus?

Marriage

If you have a choice, consider not getting married; it is difficult to understand a Venetian. But if you want to get married, marry someone from your hometown rather than someone from another country; you will have a more common ground for your marriage to blossom. Moreover, marrying someone with some commonality will reduce lots of traveling on the one hand and reduce lots of cultural misunderstandings. But, on the other hand, if you are the bold one and marry someone outside the United States, there will be benefits. You will root your family into a thousand-year-old culture and inherit priceless rich traditions to pass on to your children permanently where US History was but just a couple hundred years old.

Annual Vacations

By the time my kids were 11 and 9, they had each traveled to China at least seven times, then separately, my wife and I had traveled back also. Culturally, Chinese parents expect you to return home once per year during the Chinese New Year.

When my wife gave birth to our children, she couldn't wash her hair for ten days and needed to wash it with ginger. Then when the babies are 100 days old, you need to throw a red egg birthday party with everything red.

When the kids were born, we were supposed to request a travel visa for her parents. Grandparents need to see the babies and take care of them when they're born; it is a requirement.

Food

You must have soup before every meal. You can't drink cold water, can't drink soda, you can't have ice cubes. You must eat rice with every meal. The salad was not the in thing, neither pizza nor cheese nor hamburger; skip it. If the food is not spicy, it is bland; it's not good food, so forget it. All Chinese food here in the US is lousy as they are not authentic like my wife's hometown, she says.

Of course, we need to buy more tofu. We can't buy frozen wonton, it has to be handmade, and whatever we can't finish, we must put it in the freezer, so it doesn't spoil. So yes, we need to buy vitamins for your parents now for when you see them next year.

The vegetables must be fresh from the grocery store daily. Fish must be alive before you cook it. We can't cook with pans; we can only use a wok. We need more of this; we need to get more of that. It would be best if you had a couple of shelves full of different kinds of noodles and hot chili spices.

Health

It would be best if you kept a couple of bags of prescription black tea leaves herbs for stomach pain and other black tea leaves herbs for other health problems. The black tea leaves must be cooked in a unique pot for several hours. The house stinks afterward, but you can't say anything to your wife.

Then, of course, you must go to an acupuncturist because that's science. US massages always cost more than the $20 massage in China. You must acknowledge that China massages are the best. You must shower at night before you sleep, not in the morning. You can't wear shoes in the house; they must be hardwood floors, not carpets. Oops, that's before all the feng shui preaching, the Chinese zodiac, or the 5,000 years of Chinese history.

Imagine the rich cultural traditions my kids would have missed if I didn't marry someone from China. I never thought traditions mattered much before I married but bending to so many new rituals day after day was a lot of work. Still, it was well worth it to the kids and me when we visited China and ate all the local spicy food. The tradition was priceless, making an excellent marriage for us, as the next generation will confirm.

Raising Kids

I would give my wife more credit in this area. I would instead let my babies cry more, but the Chinese way was to pick them up, not let them cry even if the baby won't sleep. Parents don't let babies walk on their own or climb or venture; they may fall and hurt themselves. Mommy needs to hold the baby all the time. Mommy cannot let her baby run off on its own. The baby falls and scrapes their knee or gets dirt on their hands; quickly wash the germs off immediately. I would let them continue to venture and play and build their immune system. If they sneezed, mom would say, quickly, put on your jacket. If it's raining outside, mom says you can't play in the rain; you will catch a cold. Kids must go to bed early. I process this differently.

If the kids don't behave, tell them again. For example, if they don't eat what's on the table, ask them to eat again. If they make a fuss and don't listen, the same thing happens; tell them to listen.

Extracurricular Activities – Intelligence: Chemistry, Piano, Guitar, Volleyball, Soccer

We raised our kids in our Christian home, where we placed them in all sorts of extracurricular activities and allowed them to find activities that bring joy to their lives.

My daughter's childhood consists of taking Chinese classes, Piano, Guitar, Flute, and Songwriting lessons. She also participated in Soccer, Volleyball, Karate, Kumon, math tutoring, watching all her brother's sporting games, and taking photos of him and his teammates. But music was always something that stuck around, and it brought her a lot of peace.

My son's childhood consists of taking Chinese classes, Piano, Soccer, Baseball, Football, Karate, and Kumon. Sports and running in the wind make him feel alive.

Chinese classes were repetitive. Playing the Piano was a repetition. In sports, it was repetition. All of these create interest, and a desire, which are the building blocks of forming personal habits that one would be accountable for in life.

Intelligence: Chemistry, Piano, Guitar, Volleyball, Soccer

The significance of playing piano for the Chinese was vital. There are seven forms of intelligence: Bodily-Kinesthetic intelligence, Logical-Mathematical intelligence, Linguistic intelligence, Spatial intelligence, Interpersonal intelligence, Intrapersonal intelligence, and Musical Intelligence.

With Music, studies of infants suggest they would gain a "raw" computational ability in early childhood. So, we believed our kids would do well if they played piano and other musical instruments, just like my sister, brother, and me.

Stephanie definitely has Musical Intelligence. She could listen to a song and able to play the piece automatically with both hands, from complex pop music to Disney songs.

From repetitions to interests, to desires, to habits, I saw how my son, Jeremy, had leveraged that in observing patterns, learning them, and then improving on them. At the age of eight, my son would watch YouTube. If he saw someone do a bicycle kick, he was interested in doing it too. He would watch it again and again. He would visualize and rehearse it in his mind. Then one day, we went out to the backyard. On his second try, he completed a soccer bicycle kick and scored.

At age nine, my son memorized the periodic chemistry table. I reminded him that if you learn something for 20 minutes per day, it is over two hours in one week. If you continue doing that for one year, that's over 100 hours of a subject matter that you would have perfected. Based on that idea and incremental learning, he mastered the periodic chemistry table by building a daily learning habit.

Are you a hard worker? What does working hard look like?

So many realtors and loan officers tried selling real estate or closing a loan. After a few tries, they quit. So many kids try to do this, try to do that, but it doesn't work, and they quit.

How are kids' learning habits, and how are kids adjusting to reality post-Covid?

At age 10, Jeremy worked at Uncle Miller's ranch one morning, bailing hay and feeding horses at 7:30 am, and he learned all about hard work. He scraped his skins, stirred up mosquito hives by accident, got stung on his arm and forehead, and continued to work. He got his hands dirty, and he didn't complain at all. That's hard work.

But if all we do is think, visualize, and do, then does everything always happen the way we want? Would our world always be perfect?

When my daughter was 12 years old, she saw and met a volleyball USC Olympian, Nicole Davis. The USA was playing Brazil while we were vacationing in Hawaii. Something rubbed off after she got Nicole's autograph. Then my daughter wanted to play volleyball in college.

She was so scared of the ball at first; she missed the ball and the dig and worried about what people might think and say. She went through many practices and private coaching sessions and switched to four different clubs to get more play time, but she was still benched most of the time due to her size. My daughter struggles so much as a volleyball player. At five feet tall, she could only play the Libero position. She was so disappointed after every game and after every weekend. She cried so many times it was so painful for us to comfort her. Visualization did not help; habits did not help, and hard work did not help because she lacked *bodily-kinesthetic*.

She even tried out for a D1 college in Colorado and many other colleges in California, but no go. Then, finally, she fell in love with the University of Colorado, so she abandoned her volleyball dreams and only pursued academics.

My son has loved soccer since Day one. From scoring his first goal, he caught the bug. Then he went to his first out-of-town tournaments. He was like a superstar. He scored nine goals in eight games. Wow, what a joy to watch him play. He was consistent at a young age.

With some growing pains in his legs, while he was 12, it took about one season away from him; he was super bummed about the lost time, and we were too.

Then the summer before going to high school, we sent him to a two-week soccer camp in Portugal to play on the Benfica team. After two weeks, they awarded him the Rui Costa Most Valuable Player award. Again, I was surprised my son was that good internationally.

As his teammates grew older, his physique did not catch up. He was not as fast as others. Finally, he could not keep up playing forward anymore; he was then moved to a midfielder and then to defense. He was sad; we were sad for him too.

Then he wanted to work on his size and his weight. So I took him to a gym across town to work with Mario, an ex-professional soccer goalie. They trained together for over three months, and on and on we went. He was focused, worked out an hour and a half each time, and sweated repeatedly.

I wish that my son had musical intelligence; he does not. I hope that my son has Bodily-Kinesthetic Intelligence; he does not. Whenever Jeremy fell, he would say, Dad, if you have better genes, it would be easier for me to get to Division 1 Colleges.

But certainly, he did not need better genes for the minutes to hours he spent watching YouTube learning new soccer defensive moves that are better than what I can do. Instead of continuing to blame me for not having great genes, that he would be a natural soccer player, he worked at it. As a result, he developed better genes than I had.

He formed new habits for himself so that no one could question him or take the hard work he put in away from him. The minutes to hours he spent practicing soccer at home were his passion. Soccer was his love. He had even kicked the ball so hard into the wall that there were now three cracked sheetrock holes and other sheetrock screws that needed re-taping.

He now continues his workout at the gym in addition to his club practices. He's not a 6' 185lb center back, but he's got more tenacity as a 5'10, 160lb right back than most kids I know. He wants to go to a Division 1 college soccer team. He sets his mind on that; he practices and assures himself that he will get there. While he received many offers for D2 and D3, he said, Dad, I've worked too hard to settle for D2 and D3 colleges. We are proud of him and his stick-to-it pride and pursuit.

My Kids' Choices After High School

Stephanie had a challenging time in high school because most kids were into social media, and it was hard for her to know who her real friends were and who were not. She was so glad that high school was over in 2020 during covid. Stephanie did not care much about graduation; the school didn't have one, and Stephanie was OK with it. She took an IB World Religion Course, which also gave her a balanced view of religion by studying the foundation of faiths from Buddha, Confucius, Daoism, Hinduism, Judaism, Mormon, Muslim, et. al.

Stephanie received several college credits from her AP and Junior College courses. She attended the University of

Colorado with the intent to study Speech Language and Hearing Science. However, halfway through her first year, she realized this was not the career path for her.

High School did not prepare my daughter for college. As parents, we did not do a good job helping her define and envision a career path that she would pursue and stay the course.

In January 2021, instead of selling books where it had changed my life, Stephanie took a trip to LA to visit her cousin, Moses Lin, who had made it as an A-List guitarist in the LA and Orange County wedding industry. @MosesLinMusic

As she spent time with him, she reflected on the things that brought her joy. Then she thought about music and songwriting seriously. Then music or photography. Then three weeks later, after a lot of prayer about her future, she landed her first concert photography gig. Finally, Stephanie realized she could mix her love of music and photography. Well, I guess maybe as parents, we can take some credit for paying for the music lessons where she had built lifelong habits that had inspired her in music, along with the cameras we bought for her.

In September 2021, she applied for Marina William's Colorpop event, and out of hundreds of applicants, she was picked as the youngest photographer to attend the content weekend. Marina Williams was someone she had looked up to for years. Her creative eye and confident demeanor stood out to her. She spoke so much truth and encouragement over her that Stephanie decided then that, if anything, she wanted to give photography the best shot that she's got.

After Colorpop, doors began for her. First, as a freelancer, Stephanie started serving at the Red Rocks Church and Ascent Community Church photography team. Then, her habits kicked in, and she sent hundreds of emails connecting her with publicists and magazines in the music industry to get her foot in the door with concert venues.

Stephanie then landed a position with Haze Media. Then she served as the in-house photographer at Gothic Theater, covering shows for them. Stephanie then shot her first ever Red Rocks Amphitheater show and took on a Director of Photography role shooting Alec Benjamin. Then she went on a 3-day music tour with Kayla Ruby and shot photos for Eli Young's Band.

Stephanie then moved to Nashville, where she continued to chase her dream of working with music artists and towards the 50th anniversary CMA Awards in 2023. She now interns for four music artists. In addition, Stephanie will be the lead photographer for a wedding with over 500 people in December in North Carolina. She has switched colleges and will finish her BA Degree in Digital Media Literacy with Arizona State University Online by February 2023 in less than three years. Stephanie had stepped out from her shell from a very well thought out guarantee of 40 hours per week employment to an unpredictable freelance income earner at age 20. Her foundation of faith and now trusting God's plan for her was like my faith and my father's. What we believe as our calling to serve others is always greater than our personal goals.

While this may all sound glamorous, my daughter is still 20 years old, with many fears, doubts, and uncertainties about her future. And even at this age, she knows the answer to all her worries will evaporate with her next gig, next shoot, and her subsequent introductions. But all she needs to do to succeed daily is get up, attend venues and events, and meet folks at churches. And when she dialogues and connects with people in Nashville, she believes everyone is connected to someone who will help her business to take off. She just needs to meet and introduce herself, ask for an introduction, and share her Instagram with others @StephanieHSiau.

Stephanie also cracked the code with her most significant struggle and is still confidently overcoming it. There are so many talented creative photographers/content producers out there, and having your work stand out from others can always be challenging and demanding. She said, "Comparison is the thief of joy," which placed her in a position of burnout and feeling unworthy to continue creating.

With an understanding that comparison is the thief of joy, Stephanie realized that at this age, she needs to minimize how she compares herself. Her biggest lesson from this struggle has helped her mentality and creativity. That was what every photographer, videographer, and musician felt like, as everyone tried to fake it until they made it in the industry with many mental health challenges.

Stephanie has been super strong in this area because of the times she got benched playing volleyball all the time. You're too short; you're not good enough; you're not fast enough, which gave her so many mental health challenges on the one hand; on the other hand, her mental toughness increased tremendously. With repetitive habits or patterns in dealing with "self-comparison to others" repeatedly for six years daily, she has become super strong in this area. Her foundation of faith is trusting that all things will work out for her in God's time

It has been a humbling feeling for Stephanie as she shared that everyone in her industry walks through each season in their career with both confidence and insecurity. However, this has allowed her to build a community with these creative folks to support and encourage one another. Stephanie noticed when she was intentional with her needs and goals within her community, saying precisely what she wanted and what she would commit to, the more inspired and encouraged she became by the people surrounding her.

Five years from now, you will become precisely the same person as you are today except for the books you read, the audio input you receive, and the people you associate with, right? What's stopping you?

As my daughter journeys through this unknown, she continues her aspirations to be a photographer specializing in brand and content photography. Her goal was to be on staff for a few musicians and work with influencers who have no time to prepare or think of other creative content to push out to the public. Stephanie likes to creatively brand and promote what an artist does best authentically and creatively and build relationships with those she works with to better share their story with the world.

Stephanie's foundation of faith that drives her was not for the fame or the money but to be able to use her God-given creativity to love others and be a vessel of light in this interesting time in our economy within the creative/entertainment industry.

On the other hand, Jeremy just finished high school with a 4.5 GPA and was only accepted by Boston University for college. He played on the high school varsity soccer team for all four years and was co-captain in his senior year. Jeremy was MVP of the team several times and was selected as a nominee for California Regional MVP of the year. As the votes came in from his peers, he was in Second place with over 35,000 votes.

Aside from playing high school soccer, Jeremy played club soccer for over nine years. For the last 12 months, his coach only plays him as a center-back. Yet, that position he found out three months before high school graduation was that it would not give him the best advantage of being recruited due to his height and size. Jeremy did not bring that to his club coach's attention. He didn't ask them to switch him to playing right back so he would receive better-recruiting opportunities. It was humbling for Jeremy to stay in that spot as he was the best center-back player to help the team finish a winning season. That sacrifice, on the one hand, didn't help launch his sports career. On the other hand, Jeremy is my hero for his integrity based on his faith that everything would work out and he did not need to rush the process.

Despite his self-sacrifice, Jeremy continued to work after school in weight training for 1.5 to 2 hours a day, 3 to 5 times per week, along with individual tactical training. He kept his daily habits with no coaching. Jeremy knows what's required, and practice, practice, and practice. At the end of each practice, when arriving home in the garage, he would sit there for 10-20 minutes just jotting down notes from his training session where he could improve. After a game/tournament, while driving home, he would jot down more notes on his performance and how he could improve. I never have to push, encourage him, or help him set goals. He had a plan and always reminds me, Dad; you don't think I had already thought about all this; of course, I have. And he's back to YouTube, practicing, sleeping, and the same thing every day. Amazing habits.

He, too, like his sister, had taken IB World Religion. He studied other religions' rituals and beliefs, challenging him to be steadfast in his faith. He did not cave into soccer pressure. Nothing shakes his posture. He is solid as a rock in knowing his future has a place for him to be in the top 1% of soccer athletes in the United States.

As a result, after graduation, instead of going to Boston University for academics, he took a gap year to sharpen his axe more and improve his defensive right back and right winger skills.

He has gone through many out-of-state college recruiting camps like Northwestern University, Boston University, University of Memphis, University of Connecticut, and many California college tryouts. Jeremy experienced disappointments repeatedly by not being offered a spot immediately. My son would say to me: Dad, don't you think I have already thought about this? Yes, I have. And he's back practicing again when he returns home.

Recently, he told me, Dad, I'm not going to over-eat just to gain bad weight. Gaining one lb. per week is too much. It is not sustainable for an athlete to gain that much weight because the bone structure won't be able to handle it. So I am on track, gaining 1/4 lb. per week.

He wasn't sure if his new Sacramento United MLS club team and his teammates were ready for competition this year. So he took charge and invited his teammates to play in indoor pickup games. He offers to pay for all their entry fees so the team can bond better.

Jeremy's team was supposed to compete in the San Diego Surf Club in the First Bracket, but the team was placed in the Sixth Bracket instead. This placement meant recruiters would not look at him again during this tournament; as they mostly scout players in the First and Second Brackets only. Yet, Jeremy was still purposeful, with no emotion; he said he would stay with his commitment, play through the tournament, and try out at colleges directly instead.

Jeremy's commitment to play through meant repeatedly cutting videos on his own and sending videos to hundreds of D1 coaches till 4 am. Then, he calls the coaches and follows up. Not because I want him to do this, but because he does it alone, without my help and guidance. He has been quite a mature adult doing everything independently to pursue his goals without making excuses.

One of Jeremy's indispensable drives is to do everything himself, without any handouts, favors, or referrals from my friends, USC alums, or anyone I know. He wanted to do everything by himself, his way, without regrets. So, he tried to earn his spot based purely on hard work and habits driven.

When was the last time you had a setback or failed at something and just had to blame someone else? What would the outcome have been if you had wholly owned the event?

All my life, I had recruited individuals that were not initiative-taking hundreds and thousands of times, and I was so disappointed. But my kids, their choices, and the decisions they made, I am sure the good Lord above had shone his favor on our family. I don't think it is something I should take credit for, but if we put our time and effort into selflessly serving the public and being charitable, I'm confident we will all reap our rewards accordingly.

Adoption to Changes Quickly

Chapter 5

What do you do when there are significant changes in your life?

Do you go through Denial, Anger, Frustration, and Bargaining before Acceptance? Sometimes, life doesn't give you that much time. Or if you can go from Denial to Acceptance in hours or days instead of weeks and months, how much sooner will you get back on your Paths? Right?

When I got laid off from HP during the tech bubble, I wondered what I should do. Should I move back to Silicon Valley and look for work there? They were laying off there too. Should I go back to the Department of Defense, where everyone had consolidated, and move to San Diego North Island Depot? Or should I look for work in Roseville?

I believed engineering would be a slow path for the next two years, so I decided to look for something combining my Southwestern sales experience with my Industrial Engineering technical background. I had thought that the habits learned in making sales calls would benefit any bank. And as I had worked with loans on and off for the last five years, I decided to go into full-time mortgage banking for a bank.

Setting myself a 90-day clock, I mailed out my resume and followed up with phone calls. Within 30 days, I was offered employment by John Howarth at Chase Manhattan Bank. I was to start 30 days later. After previously working as a part-time mortgage broker, I did not know how the A-to-Z banking operation worked. So, I asked if I could come to work two weeks early **without pay** to be crossed trained and learn from other successful loan officers. John had agreed.

Chase Manhattan Bank

At Chase, I made copies for those first two weeks, faxed paperwork for other loan officers, and did a bunch of odds and ends. I asked questions to reduce my learning curve, like pulling credit, reading credit reports, understanding the rate sheet, and how to access, read and understand lending guidelines.

One of the reasons this position opened was because there were many clients in the bank database that no one had reached out to in a very long time. So, I was hired to cold call these people on the phone by soliciting their mortgage business as the company lost its customers to others. So, from day one, I put together my cumulative sales experience from selling books, Lehman Brothers cold calling, network marketing, and prior loan brokering training. Then, I just dialed one number after another, non-stop, every day.

My first client was a father with 12 kids who wanted a $120K loan in June 2001. Then when preparedness and opportunity met, I was so lucky. Mortgage rates dropped dramatically after 9/11. Instead of working a typical 8-hour day, I worked

14 hours a day; it was a non-issue for me as I had previously worked those hours from 8 am to 10 pm.

Fannie Mae then allowed banks to close loans without appraisal and income documentation. Since closing a full doc loan may take 90 days and a no appraisal loan may take 30 days, I would go into the office almost every Saturday. I would find the current bank's client that qualified for this program, put 8-10 loans together on a Saturday, and put the completed loan files on my processor's desk when she came in on Monday.

Reaping Habit of Successes with Mortgage Lending

After six months, I closed over $12M in production, winning the Rising Star award. In 2002, I closed over $40M. In 2003, I had closed over $75M with over 432 loans. There were months I made $50K per month. I had made over $100K a couple of times per month. I could not believe it. During the first 24 months with Chase Manhattan Bank full-time, I had closed over $100M in production. But as a W2 employee, I could not believe the amount of taxes they took out either.

Imagine closing an average of 35 loans per month, day in and day out; if I didn't understand operations like selling umbrellas, it wouldn't have worked. If I weren't an efficient-minded engineer, many customers would have complained. I would be an amateur if I didn't know how to establish rapport, answer objections, and close. Instead, it appears I was at the right place at the right time, where I could use all my talents correctly every day. What a blessing. Because of the repetitive daily habits I had built years ago, I was blessed—doing something repeatedly that saved me time and made me much faster than most others.

During those years, I had a full-time processor. I had an assistant that ordered prelim and appraisal reports. My wife assisted me with marketing, mailers, and closing letters to agents. I worked six days per week, 14 hours a day, and on weekends, I read product guidelines while holding my baby girl at night. That way, I would know the best way to explain program requirements to folks.

My processor, Dana, working with me at the time, many would consider us to be the two most unmatched individuals. She smoked all the time, took 15-minute breaks every other hour, and cussed every other sentence. But she was impressive in getting my loans into underwriting and pulling them out. So many other cordials processors did not compare to her. She was pretty awesome. She knew how to work hard and keep up.

There were times I wanted to do more production, but that required me to staff up more, but I was not willing to invest more, so that was one of my downfalls, my wife and I did almost everything.

Being recognized by Chase Manhattan Bank as the #17 producer in California and Presidents Club trips to Scottsdale Marriott Hotel retreat with over 1,000 attendees or Monterey was fun and appreciated.

While that all sounded fun and extravagant, it was a lot of work from day one. For example, how are 30 to 150 files organized monthly and submitted to a processor efficiently when there are missing items? How are communications and customer responses tracked? For example, how do you save the rates quoted and honor expired quotes? And then customers call again to get a lower rate. Or contact again to change loan programs, lower loan amounts, buy down rates, or change from impounding taxes to not impounding taxes and insurance?

Explaining impound accounts was also challenging. When everyone was refinancing and underwriting, turn time changed from three weeks to three months; keeping everyone cool and calm was a lot of work, or being a true artist while working.

I sometimes wish there were more hours in a day, but with the processing and underwriting staffing shortage, if I had hired another support staff, our loans would still not close any faster than 2 to 3 months at the time. So, the decision not to hire additional staff was the right call.

One thing I learned from my mentor Leslie when I started doing loans part-time in 1996 was to offer folks a no-cost loan. As such, when co-workers were charging folks a 6% rate and paying $5K in closing costs, I would help folks to understand that we were in a declining mortgage market. Therefore, that 6.5% rate at no closing cost would serve them better. Then in the future, we can still provide them a 5.75% rate at no closing cost again. Whereas paying $5K at 6%, no one would pay another $5K closing cost again at 5.5% next, right? As a result, when folks did not have to pay closing costs, they were ok with patiently waiting for their closing date.

Because of these techniques, many of my clients stayed with me 20 years later. I offered a concept that saved them money repeatedly with lower rates. When consumers are educated, lower interest rates are never the solution. Not having to pay closing costs was the solution to how I educated my clients, who became clients for life.

HOMEBUYING ✓ CHECKLIST

Finances

- Get pre-approved
- Create a monthly budget
- Research mortgage options
- Save for a down payment and closing costs
- Establish and maintain good credit
- Check credit score and report

Build your dream

- Find a real estate agent
- Meet with a lender

Documents

- W-2s from past year
- Pay stubs from the past 1-2 months
- proof of supplemental income
- Tax documents from the past two years
- Bank statements from the past 1-2 months
- Investment account statements
- Statements for all debts
- Copy of driver's license
- History of residence for past 2 years

Then years later, I was competing on a purchase loan, and I had to broker out the loan. And for some reason, the borrower said I had offered him a no-closing cost offer on a purchase loan. I would never have done that as there were more closing costs on a purchase loan with owner title insurance costs in the bay area and property tax transfer. So I took a big hit, paid for all his closing costs, and made $0 on that loan so that I could keep my promise to him as my client. Since then, he has refinanced, purchased, and referred many others to me as I took care of him on his home purchase; we are still friends today.

Marketing-wise, I spent many hours supporting the Sacramento Consumer Credit Counseling. I did first-time homebuyer presentations for them as community service and generated new business. In addition, I did several trade shows in Oakland Chinatown and exhibited in Sacramento on Chinese New Year's to expand our presence. I spoke Cantonese and Mandarin and assisted many non-English-speaking borrowers and buyers. I love educating home buyers; I love helping people.

I mailed out a professionally designed 4-page glossy newsletter regarding the mortgage market to my client and realtor. At Christmas time, I would mail out a music CD to realtors. Everyone received a birthday card from me on their birthday. In February, my clients received a copy of their Closing Statement to file with their tax returns. And it was a monthly or annual habit that I repeatedly did. Why? Because to me the right relationship was everything to me.

At the time, I pride myself on spending about $15,000 of my income yearly on marketing. But, being a pastor's kid, growing up in a family that did not have a lot, I was very frugal with how I spent my money and when to invest back into my business.

As a top producer, sometimes, I saw the production turn time getting longer, file flow, and customer service level not in alignment. Sometimes, my perspective was different based on my past. Then one day, 2.75 years later, there was a meeting of minds. I departed and joined John Howarth, who had moved to a large national bank with Diane Bacon.

A Large National Bank

The first week, the bank flew me to its headquarters in Minneapolis, Minnesota. Then once a week, I would work a half day in the Truckee office and a half day in the Tahoe office. I made many friends in those vacation/resort communities. I was at this bank for one year without any assistant. It was difficult for me as there was too much free time during the traveling day or the long drive. Quantity and repetition did not work for me. Driving did not work well for me, either.

Countrywide

I then received an offer to join Countrywide. It included an irrefutable cash sign-up bonus offer with a paid assistant. I was all in. Countrywide had a 'Fast and Easy' loan program similar to Chase Manhattan Bank. Income and appraisals were not required. It was fun to assist clients with loans that would save them appraisal money.

My new assistant, who had joined me, spoke mandarin, and we shared some interesting stories. Jenny had a master's degree in business. She was not working in 2004, yet she wanted to get into the loan business and start from the ground floor. Jenny had no experience in lending, so I asked her to promise that if she were to start, we would never discuss additional salary compensation for one year and that her commitment to me would be one year. She agreed.

The month after she joined me, she announced she was pregnant. A couple of weeks after that, my wife and I had two months of planned vacations to Europe and China.

With little training and pregnancy, my assistant worked long hours, putting together all my files every day just by figuring things out herself. She was able to assist with closing over $4M of loan production for me per month for both months. I was impressed. She was tired when I returned.

Of course, most everyone who worked for me felt like they could do it independently. Six months later, my assistant went on maternity leave. When she returned, she decided to be a loan officer independently while caring for her baby at home rather than being on my team. That was fine with me as I had hired another assistant after she had left. My new assistant was working out fine.

Like Jenny and many of us in the lending industry, I feel the rush. The rush gives birth to greed that sets in, having not experienced so much income all at once. We were undisciplined. We had no mentors with what to do with our careers or our money.

Career-wise, I thought doing loans and making great money was too easy. I wanted more. I wanted to do something that didn't require such a demanding workload that could create more cash flow.

Perhaps these thoughts are what produce my downfalls. Unfortunately, this was the beginning of one of my downfalls. One day, I learned there was a career opportunity. I was able to participate in the USC Recruiting Event featuring Merrill Lynch.

I got on a plane, flew to USC, and attended the event. Over 200 college seniors and new graduates showed up to learn what Merrill Lynch was about, how to join them, and the career opportunity to be a financial advisor. At the end of the evening, like everyone shaking the speaker's hands, I shook Steve's hand too and got his business cards.

The following day, I called Steve and told him my flight was leaving later this afternoon and asked if I could come in and meet for an information interview and learn who I would need to speak with in Sacramento. So, an hour later, we met face to face.

Then I told Steve that at age 19, I did one of the craziest things 99% of all college students would not do. I hitchhiked from Santa Clara to Santa Barbara to Cal Poly and drove across the country to Nashville for a one-week sales school training to learn how to sell books and bibles door to door to families with kids.

I told him how I would make presentations in 20 minutes increments and present 30 times per day. Then told him how I worked six days a week and spoke to over 180 families per week and over 5,000 families per summer to sit down with over 2,000 families. And I had done that for three summers in North Carolina, Maryland, and Virginia to pay my way through USC.

I asked Steve, "Who should I talk to in Sacramento, and which position should I fill in Sacramento?"

Steve then said to me, "Wow!" which sounded incredible. "Stay here for a second."

Then, two minutes later, he asked me to go to a meeting room, where he gave me an aptitude test to complete in 30 minutes. He then returned and gave me a second aptitude test that took an hour. We then shook hands, and I left with the Managers contact info in Sacramento to follow up.

A couple of days later, when I checked in with Steve on the phone, he told me. "Of the 200 people who showed up at the recruiting event, you were the only one who called and followed up. You showed the boldness and initiative that no one else exerted. No one was quite as ready as you when I met you at the office."

I smiled as that was just music to my ears.

I then spoke to the Sacramento manager, who gave me specific instructions. I had to call, ask, talk to, and interview at least three financial advisors before they made a decision. I did, and two weeks later, they presented an offer to me.

Because of my selling books door to door sales experience and my mortgage book of business that I had built, they recognized that my habits were tough to find or train someone new in this industry. Then in 2007, they offered to accept me into their Merrill Lynch 2-year training program. I was required to come to work at 7:00 am each day and study until 4:00 pm. I would do that each day for two years to pass the Series 7, 66, Life Insurance, and the Certified Financial Planner 6 parts course. With zero sales production requirements or obligations, Merrill Lynch would pay me $100,000 yearly to sit, learn, take, and pass all the tests. Of course, I said yes; I left Countrywide and began immediately.

Merrill Lynch

Getting up each day was easy; driving and studying were easy, like studying for my five parts real estate broker test, GRI, Tax, or notary. Taking the sample tests was quite challenging as they were standardized tests. Over the years, I developed good daily habits. I did not need to drink coffee to keep awake, I did not drink alcohol to put myself to sleep, and I did not complain over the volume of material to regurgitate. I did not complain about self-studying everything by myself. If this was what I was supposed to do, I just did what my employer asked me to do every day as best as I could with zero lip service. Right?

After six months of studying, I was cramming one week before taking the Series 7 Federal exam.

Then the day before my Series 7 exam, I was pretty stressed, cramming so much data and details in such a brief period in my brain that I developed shingles in my back. Was this another sign from God?

Then I considered these thoughts, "If this kind of work created so much stress that it produced shingles, would it be worth it in the future? Would I be better off leveraging my current mortgage client and moving them to be asset clients and build a brand-new book of business, or would I rather go back to mortgage lending as it was less stressful without creating a new book of business?

After I passed my Series 66 and insurance license, I gave notice that I was giving up the balance of my 24 months of training pay as I needed to work with less stress in my life.

The final week I was at work, Merrill Lynch stocks went from $90 to $30. The weeks after I left, the financial mortgage housing bubble took shape unbeknownst to me from July 2007 to 2011.

Companies were laying off people just like in 1987, just like in the 2001 Tech Bubble, but now, homes were going upside down in value, and people were foreclosing on their homes. Lehman Brothers then collapsed, which I had worked for before. Next, Bearn Stearns collapsed, and many banks laid off loan officers.

I only remember that I needed to go to work and build consistency in something. If you ask 100 people if they are hard workers, all 100 people would say yes. To me, hard work or working hard means working the hours. Working 10-14 hours per day, then that's hard work every day. Otherwise, you are just clocking in time and waiting for a paycheck.

I worked hard, 10-14 hours every day. I told myself daily since I knew I didn't want to be a financial advisor. I knew now that I wanted to be a loan officer and must do all the loan officer's daily activities. I had given up $140K of my money over the next 1.5 years, and I better not be stupid and not make that back. I knew I needed to be a solid loan officer that exceeded this trade-off.

Before joining Merrill Lynch, doing loans became mundane after closing over 750 loans, but guess what? Success is boring, I realized. To be successful, you keep doing and doing and doing the same thing over and over again, whether you like it or not.

A successful person does what an unsuccessful person is not willing to do. Don't wish it were easier; wish you were better. — John Rohn

Guild Mortgage

I then hung my Series 7 License with Plan Well Live Well as their in-house mortgage lender. I joined a local net branch of Guild Mortgage and did residential and commercial loans. The broker was innovative as he purchased leads, who then forwarded the inbound leads to us on a live transferred call. I did not get it; I was not used to the slow process and the poor quality of the leads he provided. The leads were coming like one every 10 minutes to an hour. I couldn't develop the correct repetition or build a good habit to see any success. I was there for a short time and did not get good at working inbound leads. If you're talking to two people per hour, and at the snap of a second, you had to give 15 seconds or one-minute sales pitches for only a couple of hours a day, it was different from the number of calls in a concise time frame than getting better with each phone call. I did not get the correct results and could not build good habits in a broker world. So I decided to search for better opportunities.

First Horizon Home Loans

Following Guild Mortgage, I joined John Howarth for the third time at First Horizon Home Loans. In February 2008, few folks were looking to purchase or refinance a home that year due to the market crashing. Did I make a mistake in departing Merrill Lynch?

Once on board, I learned new tools, marketing, and construction loan programs. Then, in the daytime, I called, emailed, sent birthday cards, prepared marketing materials, set up first-time home buyers' presentations, and set up realtor presentations on sellers' concessions to show realtors how they looked. Not much production in 2008, which was probably my worst year.

Then at the end of 2008, I felt like my third summer selling books. After I left Merrill Lynch, if the guaranteed income was a yardstick of measurement, I had failed as I did not earn the income if I had stayed at Merrill Lynch. Did I make the right choice or not?

2009, I was sure I had to ramp up as the real estate market may start to turn positive. The only thing I knew I needed to do was to go on a guerrilla marketing hunt as fast as I could for as long as I could. So, I started to gather my client and prospect list. Then I remembered what I had said a couple of years ago in an interview.

Mortgage Originator Magazine interviewed me in Sept 2002 as a Rookie Superstar. I remember my quote: "when you boil it down to the essence, one of two things needs to happen every day: either the phone rings and someone wants you to be their loan consultant, or you create enough activities so that your phone rings. That's my job every day, that's why I'm here, that's what I'm supposed to do every day."

After that, I revised my mantra and said it to myself daily to get myself going. In a concise, repeated habit, I need to call as many people as fast as I can every day and night. For example, if I could issue a closing cost proposal to 10 people, two people would say yes. So I kept at it, repeatedly calling folks until 8 pm. At the end of the year, my 2009 production was 600% higher than my 2008 production volume.

As I touched base with many folks in my database, one of my past clients referred me to his partner, and we looked to refinance his $13 M property. Unfortunately, the two appraisals didn't substantiate the property value, but I had fun trying.

I based my decision to contact previous clients on the awareness of a down market. In other words, get to work,

Joe. I knew how to make the call and knew what to say. I had learned how to put a loan together. I just needed to work non-stop with as many folks as possible and as fast as possible to talk to them to generate inertia. Then from inertia to momentum, then to a few closings, to more closings, without thinking, without stopping, wondering, wishing, and asking why. The third summer selling books was a great reminder of how I need to bounce back from failure; you must have a plan.

I never got answers from asking why in the past. I had asked why my umbrellas had taken 35 years to rid of them. No answers came when I crashed my car or the many times I didn't recruit more than two college students to sell books. I asked why no answers came. I had asked why when my network marketing business didn't grow. I needed to just tuck the "why questions" between my legs, shut up and just work, work, and work. I just needed to stop asking all the nonsense "why's" each time. Working hard is the best solution. I needed to put myself into a habit of working long hours if I was ever in doubt. Working hard means working 10-14 hours daily to get that momentum in my favor.

MetLife

In 2010, MetLife acquired our bank. We now had the excellent Snoopy Brand, *"Making Dreams Come True 365 Days a Year."* Who doesn't like Snoopy? On one particular March, the bank ran a *"March the Madness"* contest to meet as many realtors as you could. I guess I like contests. I came in second place and won a pocket-size video recorder before the iPhone was popular. I did it by visiting many open houses and meeting many realtors, some of whom are still my friends today, and I still receive phone calls from them every so often.

During this period, I needed an assistant. The good Lord above must have shone his beacon of light on me. Along came Dee, who was also looking to be a loan officer assistant. She previously was a top producer ranked in the nation as one of the Top 200 producers in the United States. Dee took a break from the business a few years back and decided to return to the mortgage business to join a team. She joined my team, and we were rocking and rolling. Dee helped take care of all the loans in process while I generated additional new relationships everywhere. She allowed me to work at the KB Home Builder site and speak with first-time homebuyers. She freed up some of the time so that I could spend more time with my family.

Met Life also trained me to be a Reverse Mortgages Specialist. I had partnered with a friend to do Reverse Mortgage Seminars. I was so glad I could learn and do Reverse Mortgages. I have been doing them since 2011.

As a national lender, I requested a bank-owned real estate (REO) that was previously foreclosed and offered it as a charity auction item to support The Asian Real Estate Association of America & Foundation (AREAA). As a result, we raised $4,200 for their cause.

MetLife then decided to get out of the mortgage lending business. They offered a retention bonus if we waited for management to put the pieces together to merge with another bank. But management promises were not valid promises. MetLife did get out of the mortgage lending business, but they just shut down and closed their mortgage business, and we were all out of a job; they did not merge. So instead of merging in 2012, someone moved my cheese again, and I had to look for new employment. Dee and I also decided to go our separate ways, as she wanted to return to the industry as a producing loan officer instead.

A Large Mortgage Banker

I then went to a Large Mortgage Banker working in a local Net Branch with a sign-on bonus. I had then independently paid $1,000 to have my name be on all the top search engines, where if you google Joe Mortgage Roseville, I would always be #1.

Then the craziest thing happened. A few months later, the mortgage banker was not staffed sufficiently with underwriters and closers. So, to compensate, the company approved funding for all purchase loans, but in June, they restricted that five days were not eligible for refinancing funding. Then in July, seven days were not eligible for refinancing funding. August, it was like ten days were not eligible for refinancing funding. Then September, 12 days were not eligible for refinancing funding.

Podium Mortgage

The branch manager decided that we needed to move to another bank to work instead. We decided to move to one of the Podium Mortgage Net branches. My commute since working at Chase Manhattan Bank had always been less than 1.5 miles from my home. This new location was my longest commute, two miles from home - LOL.

Then the second official start date, they told me not to come into work because the bathroom had a 6-inch water pipe burst. The entire first floor and all our file boxes were soaked; it will take a couple of weeks to replace the carpet before we can start working at the office again. Water/flooding, another sign from God? Like short selling house on fire or shingles on my back. Hum, or just like crashing my car in Maryland, off schedule again, ugh, life.

How do I get back on schedule? I remember meeting another manager that worked at another Podium Mortgage Net Branch. I contacted him, and two days later, I moved from one branch to another three blocks down the street and closer to my home. For a change, I liked my friendly, helpful manager, Tim. He was instrumental in helping me get familiar with their operation process and locating the proper support.

After I started, loans came in from past clients referring me, and I reached out every day. Every day, it felt like so many more guidelines had changed. Some days, my assistant did not collect all items required for the initial loan submission. As many folks reviewed our files, the delays got longer. How do I get files through faster? I had to sharpen my axe. I created checklists to catch missed items before going into processing and underwriting. I talked to my assistant, checked in with my processor, and collaborated. I tried to understand the new process because the processor and underwriter do not sit in my office; they work remotely in various locations.

Then we closed a purchase loan in 12 days for one realtor, and I was happier. Then one of my clients referred me to his

CEO. The next thing I knew, he had laid out 4.5 inches of tax returns on my desk. The CEO had over 170 residential and commercial properties and wanted to refinance five properties. It all sounded great, except we had to broker out his loan due to the number of residential properties he owned. The broker also required the 170 addresses, mortgage statement, tax statement, and insurance for all properties to be listed correctly on the loan application's REO (Real Estate Owned) section. That took several weeks to compile.

My poor assistant was so patient as we went through the submission process. Unfortunately, the broker channel took too long; their communications were slow as they were in New York. The broker ended up funding the five loans and kept the rate as quoted, even with the delays. All parties were glad as all loans had closed.

Then many folks who had completed their two years of bankruptcy were interested in qualifying for FHA (Federal Housing Administration) loan or asking for a new loan four years after foreclosure completion. So again, we went through other broker channels, but there were delays as many borrowers were trying to finance with that program simultaneously.

One day, the Sacramento district attorney served me with a subpoena. A husband and wife had applied for a loan with me previously. The husband asked me to repull their joint credit when his wife had a restraining order against him. I didn't know. Then he asked me for a copy of their joint credit report. I provided it to him. He used the credit report to trace down his wife's address. Although the husband had lied about his relationship status, my communications were correctly documented. We implemented new company policies to avert events like this in the future. In addition, it was against company policies to provide credit reports to borrowers in the future.

I won the Presidents Club Trip for our net branch one year later. I did not go, as it was just to Napa. I stayed and worked that day. They had a couple of awards events in Reno, and I attended those. Like with Southwestern Company, I had an itch around the third year. Should I continue working here or work somewhere else?

Provident Bank

Lightning strikes twice! The bond between John Howarth and my friendship with him was solid. In 2015, he asked me to join him at Provident Bank, so for the fourth time, I went to work for him. Although, as I now have learned, we live in a relatively small lending community, let alone working for someone twice, I was working for John for the fourth time, and Diane Bacon was my sales manager the second time.

While the industry had already moved into paperless origination, Provident Bank was still old school. For example, they still printed the entire tax returns, W2, Paystubs, and all your signed applications and addendums. They would then stack them in the correct order, make photocopies of the whole file, ship one file to the underwriter to review and keep the copy package file at the office – very old school.

Yes, that's what we did every day. We did loans and had assistants to help us stack the files and make copies, and we did that every day. With the roll-out of TRID, where Loan

Estimates were provided first, then documents eSigned or wet signed, and then appraisals were ordered. The file was then processed so closing Disclosures could go out, which had to be eSigned or wet-signed before loan docs could be released. Wow, that was a lot of work when TRID rolled out.

Sometimes I was glad we were doing the loans with all hard copies only, as technologies had failed so many times that consumers did not know how to click open or create a username/password or remember their password. Or they did not get the password reset email because it showed up in their spam or junk mail half the time. With too much technology and no one to handle technical support after hours, you would be shut down until the next day.

Then solar became a consumer benefit or a lender/realtor's nightmare. I saw an opportunity and did my research; as the Provident Bank portfolio loan did not require solar subordination, I invited realtors to a Presentation on MPower Solar. Over 23 realtors showed up, and some of

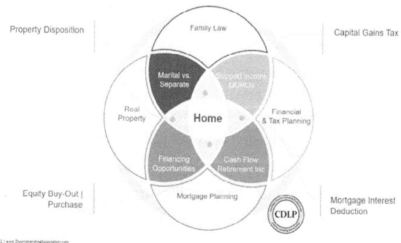

Intersection of Divorce, Real Estate & Mortgage Planning

them are still my friends today.

Provident Bank's portfolio program could also do bridge loans when they listed departure residents' sales on the MLS. Then the buyer could buy in advance.

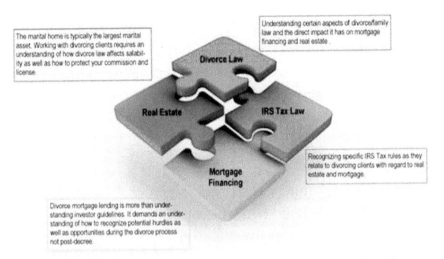

The marital home is typically the largest marital asset. Working with divorcing clients requires an understanding of how divorce law affects salability as well as how to protect your commission and license.

Understanding certain aspects of divorce/family law and the direct impact it has on mortgage financing and real estate.

Divorce Law

Real Estate

IRS Tax Law

Recognizing specific IRS Tax rules as they relate to divorcing clients with regard to real estate and mortgage.

Mortgage Financing

Divorce mortgage lending is more than understanding investor guidelines. It demands an understanding of how to recognize potential hurdles as well as opportunities during the divorce process not post-decree.

As I looked back, there was a reason I joined Provident Bank. One of my colleagues mentioned that she worked with many divorce folks in La Brea. I investigated it. Then I joined the Divorce Lending Association and became a Certified Divorce Lending Professional. Then I started meeting attorneys at the Sacramento State Bar. I presented at the State Bar for Family Law Attorneys on how to work with folks going through a divorce and how to Divorce their Mortgage with an Equity Buyout or purchase homes after a divorce. Finally, someone referred me to join the Sacramento Collaborate Divorce Group. Because of my initiatives, I became the collaborative champion and man of the year. After that, the board approved me to be the Recruiting & Membership Chair.

I was fortunate at the year-end; I made it to President's Club and the trip to Las Vegas. But, unfortunately, shortly after I had returned, many people, one by one, left the bank, retired, or were fired.

In Oct 2017, my father was not in good health. My father had fallen and hit the back of his head. After admitting him to the hospital, he didn't look well or feel well while waiting for a bed and the doctor. After being put on oxygen, he developed a mild case of pneumonia. I was told to come to Taiwan to see him. So, I went back to Taiwan and was by my father's bedside every day for ten days. He didn't get any better but did not get any worse.

After returning, things were not any better at Provident Bank. My father passed two weeks later. He was also a writer who had published many books. This book is a dedication to him five years later, how everything had turned out great with our family because of our faith.

Shortly after, I joined Diane Bacon for the third time at Homeowners Financial Group.

As you can tell, the mortgage business is not what it's all cracked up to be, right? There's always drama. There are always closing delays, and there are always processor and underwriter shortages, delays, and reductions in force. How would you like your world to be like ours, along with a 100% commission income based solely on the relationship you built with others? Then they would refer new business to you. And there is always someone backstabbing you or others lurking behind the scenes?

I have seen two managers competing for one VP position where one would oust the other to achieve his objectives. I have seen an outside CEO recruited to join the bank just to bring in his friends and then start dismissing managers who were producing managers. I have seen bad processors and bad underwriters who kept their jobs. I have witnessed the assistant stealing the loan officer's database of contacts, etc. But, overall, I credit my experience with the Southwestern company, building good habits, working the hours, and developing the habits of success that allowed me to stay ahead while switching industries and switching back to banking.

Homeowners Financial Group

Homeowners Financial Group was a different culture. The night before I went to Arizona for training, a 95% purchase loan had crashed with another big bank lender. My Top Realtor, Connie Van, asked me to assist and save the deal. First, I restructured the loan correctly so that it would underwrite. Then I went to training, and the loan was conditionally approved while I was at training. Upon returning, the appraisal was received. We closed the loan in 10 business days. It was an incredible event in the history of my loan submission. Another lender couldn't close it, and I didn't touch the file much as I was in training. Homeowners' support staff, assistance, processing, and underwriting were excellent and top-notch. This type of excellence happened repeatedly. Not that we didn't have any complex files, but we had plenty of demanding and challenging files. But everyone from my assistant to managers chipped in to put the deals together to close on time.

In 2018, business was slow across the industry again. In 2019, an opportunity came. Asian Real Estate Association of America put on a Dubai Trip for realtors and lenders. The cost was $599 for five days of hotels, food, and transportation, to all the tradeshows and events. The price included a four-hour. Real estate course and testing that allowed us to sell real estate in Dubai if we wanted to. Our only out-of-pocket expense was Airfare. I said yes when many of my friends had turned it down. It was the best time I had had in my whole life. I invited my friend Steve, a non-realtor, to join me just one week before departure. He was just in Dubai one year ago. He saw our itinerary and booked a ticket right away. He seized the opportunity when many chose not to, just like opportunities in life.

We had so much fun throughout our time in Dubai. Superb buffet breakfasts were served at the hotel each morning, along with lunch and dinners provided as we toured Dubai for our 50 attendees. We went to the tallest building in Dubai, Burj Khalifa, toured the Palm Island and Ferrari Museum properties, visited the Mosques, rode a camel, and ate a camel burger.

In 2019, I was more familiar with our broker channels. My client, who had the 170 properties, now wanted to refinance his five properties again, but now he had over 200 properties. Like prior refinancing, the broker wanted all 200 properties listed on the loan application with matching accurate expenses. Again, my fantastic assistant did all the data entries with a smile.

Just refinanced! | **$14,500,000 CASHOUT NEWPORT BEACH, CA**

"When appraisal value came in $3.0M lower than expected, Joe Siau's perseverance, dedication and problem solving skills in the super jumbo market got us across the finish line." - L.N.

Homeowners FINANCIAL GROUP — Joe Siau NMLS#582917 • JoeMortgageTeam.com

Then I started providing 100% bridge loan financing for my clients again. In fact, beyond 100%, financing was possible if one could document their income and allow a deed to be recorded on to their departure residence. We had 12 months of bank statement programs where tax returns were not required. Then we closed a 5% down purchase financing with 12 monthly bank statements with income from three businesses. In one transaction, when the home for sale was listed, we had an investor willing to allow cash-out refinancing without taking the property off MLS. So, we closed on a $1.6M jumbo cash-out loan when the property was listed for sale at $2.8 M. But my most incredible transaction that many banks could not do was a $14.55M cash-out refinance. It was a ridiculous and impossible transaction. It was the largest stated income loan closed by any loan officers in Placer County. The client's FICO was below 700. The borrower did not file US Tax Returns income. He is a US citizen, but all income and business ownerships were from outside the United States. Two appraisals came in. One was $3 M less than expected, and the other was $4M less than market value. When that happened, I called over 30 investors. I checked to see if they could accommodate the same loan amount with a 1st mortgage or 1st and a 2nd mortgage when the value dropped $4 M. It was a lot of work to convince investors that there were no extra added risks to them on a declining luxury home market.

What was the benefit of refinancing a super jumbo loan? The borrower could take out around $2.0M cash, save $20K monthly on his monthly mortgage payment, and have many of their bills and taxes paid at closing. Wow, that was the most challenging and amazing escrow I had closed up until now. I was saving someone $20K per month. Wow! And we still closed the transaction with a rate of less than 5%.

Most of all, I could still provide Reverse Mortgages to clients. And I was the preferred Reverse Mortgage Specialist in our company for California. I love educating the 55 and older folks; working here was an added benefit.
Or when a buyer is purchasing a home paying all cash, the Home Equity Conversion Mortgage for a Purchase Loan requires less cash out of pocket and no monthly mortgage payment required, just like a Reverse Mortgage; I love educating them.

Or when folks are going through a divorce, I love being a Certified Divorce Lending Professional who can assist folks

YOU DECIDE HOW TO USE REVERSE MORTGAGE PROCEEDS:
· Pay for medical costs
· Make home improvements
· Cover unexpected expenses

homeowners

HOMEOWNERS 55 AND OLDER:

Get cash from your home with no monthly mortgage payment!

With a HomeSafe loan, you don't have to wait until you're 62 to qualify for the benefits of a reverse mortgage.

· Higher loan limits (up to $4 million) than government-insured HECM loans with similar features and protections.

· Proceeds pay off your current mortgage with the remainder going to you as cash.

· Competitive rates with no mortgage insurance or out-of-pocket funds required beyond the appraisal (except for purchase).

· Must be 55 or older*, have some equity, continue to pay property taxes and homeowners insurance, and uphold the terms of the loan to keep the title to your home.

No monthly principal-and-interest payment + cash in hand = a home loan you can feel great about.

Contact me today to get started!

*For certain HomeSafe products only. Excludes MA, NY, and WA (minimum age is 60) and NC, TX, and UT (minimum age is 62). Other restrictions and guidelines apply.

with an equity buyout loan or see if a divorcee should buy a home pre-divorce or post-divorce. Equity buyout loans or purchasing a new home is helpful because alimony and child support income may not be counted as income immediately by underwriters post-divorce.

Locally, we support Bring Change to Mind, a local charity dedicated to reducing teenage suicide in Northern California, and many local food banks and charities.

Homeowners Financial Group flies everyone to Phoenix yearly for our annual State of the Union. It was incredible that a bank would do that and invest it into its people like that. Comraderies like that are essential to seeing and hanging out with other loan officers and closers you had gone through so much together. They were from all across the country, and this was extremely rewarding. Homeowners Financial Group is a great lender that takes care of its people. I learned a lot from my colleagues during these events and felt appreciated.

Not everything was perfect all the time in my world. In the beginning, my client database lacked many details. My assistant was doing manual data entries from scratch, then she didn't save the database once and had to start from the beginning again.

My support staff had health, family, relationship, income, or life issues. I had to be empathetic and let them work through their seasons in life. Then there were loan submission metrics that were always important to me to drive files to close on time. How do we make the loan process easier for our clients? How do we clear underwriting conditions faster? How do we provide final loan approval when everything is appraisal dependent?

Homeowners Financial Group has one of the best technologies in the industry. Many new social media applications with live instructions made it easier to click through to learn than I had previously experienced. Response time to a marketing request completed within one or two days was incredible.

Loan officers have access to MBS Highway, Mortgage Coach, Surefire and Total Expert, which are pretty awesome. Then added to the repertoire was Bomb, Bomb, a Google-approved web page, iMovie, and many more.

The company also paid for the Certified Mortgage Advisors Certification (CMX) for President's Club qualifier in 2019. As President Club members, we enjoyed business retreats to Sedona, Laguna Beach, Hawaii, and Park City, UT.

Covid

During the Covid shutdown, in one way, it was like 9/11. First, there was an uncertainty period of a few days; then, the mortgage rates started falling.

It was also like 2008. Many homes sat on the market without buyers for a while—fears set in with declining home prices when foreclosed homes came back on the market. Home prices kept falling. Then like a frenzy, everyone started to buy foreclosed homes everywhere in 2010, and people began to purchase homes during covid with masks on or buying homes un-seen.

On the banking side, mortgage rates increased as there were unintended consequences when the feds kept purchasing too many mortgage-backed securities right after the lockdown. Because of that, the banks' prior interest rate hedging was turning to cost banks millions of dollars each day when the Feds overreacted too quickly. When

overreacting too quickly, lower rates meant banks had to give up the money they had paid to hedge for loans scheduled for delivery at higher interest rates. The market responded well when the Fed reduced $100M of mortgage bank securities purchases to $35M to $50M monthly. Mortgage companies did not need to take such quick losses right away. Then interest rate started to decline a month later and continued for about 1.5 yrs. When that happened, it was a bottleneck everywhere with all banks. The lending industry had more loans, and everyone was short on processors and underwriters. With us, we still prioritized purchase loans ahead of refinancing.

Reaping the Habit of Success
Switching Industry and Back to Banking

The net effect, 2019, 2020, and 2021, I made President's Club three years in a row. My team and I are beyond honored. We were recognized as one of America's top 1% Mortgage Originators in 2020 and 2021. And Top 10 in customer service at my company in 2020 and 2021. We

appreciate the opportunity to compete at this level two years in a row after patiently improving for two decades. None of this could have happened if I had given up along the way. Right?

I was not saying I became the #1 loan officer in the United States. I am not. In fact, from where I am to the very top, it still appears unfathomable to me. How do I do eight times the production when there are so many daily challenges?

There are solar, appraisal, rate lock, or guideline challenges to solve every day. None of my days are ever perfect. However, each rejection, each objection, and each conversation have been a character-building experience for me as HOMEOWNERS are the reasons for everything we do and achieve.

Post-COVID

Back to working in the office was possible in late 2021— homeowners who thought about purchasing a home or refinancing met with many economic surprises to assess. Dock workers did not go to work; truck drivers did not go to work during the pandemic, which resulted from hundreds of container ships parked by the ports and unable to unload international goods. As a result, the US economy suffered from low supplies on the shelf. One popular missing item was computer chips for cars. Because without them, new vehicles could not come off assembly lines. Computer chips were lacking for new phones and computers. In fact, some rental cars were selling for the same price as new vehicles. Then there was the Russian Invasion of Ukraine which drove up worldwide tension and oil prices. France's commercial electricity price hit 1,000 euros per MWh. And there were mortgage payments not paid to China's Evergrande Development. Home prices had increased monthly, with a 15-20% appreciation average for two years straight. Had home prices peaked? Should people continue to buy houses?

US inflation topped 9.1% in June 2022. California gas prices topped $6.29 on June 30, 2022.

From Dec 14, 2021, to June 14, 2022, in six months, consumer mortgage rates went from 3.125% to 6.125%. Then Feds reacted to lagging data by increasing the prime rate from 3.25 to 6.5 in September 2022. The worst that any of us had seen in the last four years.

On the demand side, consumers were worried not enough goods would be available for them in the future; they consumed, stocked up extra, some hoarded, and some stole if they were poor. All of this increased prices for many consumable goods in the earlier days.

Cascading of events reduced consumer confidence and the desire to refinance as mortgage rates were higher. Now that home prices had peaked, buyers did not want to overpay. Home prices increase monthly, with 15-20% appreciation two years in a row. The Fed Fund's Rate increase and higher interest rates slowed consumer home purchase demands. Many banks and mortgage bankers started to lay off from 100s to thousands and 5,000s.

On July 18, 2022, National Mortgage News reported that Wells Fargo's 2021 to 2022 second-quarter earnings had fallen by more than $1.0B. Better Mortgage reported 1st quarter loss of $327M and had reduced 73% of the workforce. Loan Depot reported 1st quarter loss of $91M and will reduce its workforce by 4,800 by year-end.

It was projected by 2022; the mortgage industry production may fall by 50-60%. I also had three Loan Officer Assistant changes from October to March 2022 due to above market conditions; now, with the reduction in force, I was down to 1 assistant.

So how will I re-invent myself again? What foundation of faith can I draw on from my past? What ideas can I draw from my past? What habits can I take from my past? The purpose of this book is for me, and many of us, to know where we need to re-invent!

My Story is not your story. Your story is not my story. So what will your story be?

There are always challenges in all we do. What we do to go forward each day matters. When I was at the Department of Defense, I got the rug pulled from under me; what did I do? What did I do when Hewlett-Packard experienced a downside? What did I do? What did I do when I chose to be a mortgage lender instead of Merrill Lynch?

With higher mortgage rates, this meant that for a couple of months, the market would have many confused buyers, disappointed listing agents, and loan officers chasing realtors for business. I did not want to pursue business during the chaos. My business was about being a problem solver, a resource for everyone, and a beacon of hope.

New Adoptions, New Niches, Social Media, Technologies

I put myself on a 90-day clock to sharpen my axe to continue attracting business as a #ProblemSolvingPro. So, with the collaboration of Steve Carpenter and a financial advisor, we put together the local first ADU (Accessory Dwelling Unit) presentation from a realtor and a lender's perspective. Accessory Dwelling Units allow homeowners to put a 1200 square feet unit in Placer or a 1,000 SF unit in other counties that's financeable to improve the housing situation in California on a fast-track process with CA SB9.

I re-educated myself and continued to provide reverse mortgages to folks with a property value up to $8.0 M. Previously, the age requirement was 62, but now it is 55 to qualify.

I completed my eight hours of mortgage NMLS and 20 hours of Real Estate Broker Continued Educational course requirement.

I had dedicated myself to mastering Mortgage Coach, Bomb Bomb, and Mortgage Matter weekly videos to assist with client communications.

Most of all, I decided to author this book. Although most people and I sometimes have a 3-year goal, occasionally a 90-day plan, I decided to write the first draft in 30 days. And this was the by-product of breaking down an impossible task into daily increments and writing after 5 pm and on weekends only, never during working hours.

In other words, how can I be a leader that asks people to improve their daily habits when I alone cannot do what I say I will do? Yes, you can write the 1st draft of a book in 30 days; I did it, like Roger Bannister. In the next 90 days, I will locate a publisher and proofreaders to put this to the final version. I aim to launch this book by my father's 5th anniversary, his time in heaven.

So instead of worrying about where my business will be in 90 days, I believe I will leapfrog above my competition. When most lenders tell realtors how their rates are lower and that they should use them, I separate myself as an author with a definable track record and a subject matter expert in residential financing. In addition, realtor reading my book will agree that my vision is something they will support.

Continuing to support my mortgage business and with continuous referrals will make it possible for me to re-direct my donation dollars. Giving this book away to teens, kids in foster systems, kids with single parents, and folks in prison will build a better, safer, more entrepreneurial community for all of us. In addition, it may support a welfare system to encourage recipients to go out, try, take risks, and fish every day, month, and year for themselves. I'm honored we can show folks how to fish – with hard work. Your consumer dollars matter, and who you choose as a lender matters! I feel honored and privileged if we can partner in this cause—the #NextGenerationMatters.

As the US went into recession on July 1, 2022, due to the two years and the ten years Treasury yield curve indicators had inverted, where the two-year interest rate will earn you a higher rate of return than a 10-year interest rate. This may signify that the mortgage interest rate may be lower one day. So, while production numbers in 2022 for all loan officers and myself may be below par, I look forward to our fun times and adventures together in the next three-year cycle when we work our way to the top of our game again when rates fall below 4.5%.

Bold, Audacious Goals with Hair on it

I chose to author a book for myself. What will be your big audacious goal? I had gone to a seminar promoted by Tom Daves and Brent Gove. Seven days later, I put it out there publicly on Facebook that I would author this book. Thirty days later, I finished the first draft of this book. Will this book be published 60 days later? If you want your world to change, what are you willing to do about it? What can you do that everyone will think is impossible? Then, as you apply arduous work habits, you can say you did it!

If you continue doing the same thing you've been doing for the last year, how can you expect a different result?

Previously, I had patterned my journeys, habits, and success based on 90 days. I was marching with Santa Clara Drum and Bugle Corp, selling books on the East Coast for three months, Continental Singer for three months Tour, going from HP to Chase Manhattan Bank, and Guerilla marketing after returning to the mortgage business.

Please don't get the wrong idea. Having a goal doesn't mean you shut the world out. During the last 90 days, I did the following: I went on our President Club Trip to Park City, Utah. I took my son to the Universities of Memphis and Connecticut for soccer tryouts. I took my son to San Diego and Davis to a soccer tournament. I witnessed my son graduating high school, then attended a title officer retirement party and a realtor fundraiser. I also attended three additional charity events with CASA, Placer Community Foundation, and Acres of Hope. In addition, I attended the local Placer County Association (PCAR) Master Club event as a sponsor and presented at PCAR my Lenders Report. When my financial advisor called me to join him for breakfast and happy hour, and he would pay, I joined him. When the Insurance agent called and wanted to buy me lunch, I joined him. When my realtor called me, he wanted to buy me lunch, and another wanted to treat me to happy hour; I joined them. And when my friend Randy offered to take my son and me fishing at Ice House, we went. All the while taking some time off to go through physical therapy to work through my bursitis while authoring this book at night and swimming 7 miles per month.

Oh, I forgot to mention, because my wife was away for the last 45 days to visit my daughter, I decided to do something bold to curtail myself being just average and just chasing realtors for business. So, like not watching TV for a year, I turned off the noise instead of turning towards alcohol or other addictions and channeled my energies here. And the additional time investment I spent with my athletic son, groceries shopping, cooking for him to feed his 1500 calories plus per day, cleaning, and washing was priceless.

While setting an example for my son, he received a verbal offer to play Division 1 Soccer at this writing. Achieving this goal meant his Foundation of Faith, his visualization, his adaptions to many soccer-playing styles and ideas, and his never-ending practice had set him apart to be the Top 1% of collegiate athletes in the United States. Like me, we are both honored.

Working Hard

Not that you don't work hard. Not that you don't know how to work hard. But how do you overcome the defeated feeling when you run into challenges, are disappointed, and are flat on your face? How do you get back on your feet and gain inertia and momentum to do something? Or how do you shorten the time from disappointment to action to success? When you're out of breath, how do you get back up? Success is never a 100% sure thing all the time. There will always be difficulties in your life as there was disappointment in mine. What do we do? How do you get from point A to point B? We always have ideas. Can we continue working 10-14 hours in the short term or long term for our future? Can we agree to continue to augment our thinking and be teachable through daily learning? Can we agree to foster new associations and friendships with those who are above our ambition level?

After this book is published, I will need to apply the same habits referenced to all areas of my life to re-tool, sharpen my axe, re-invent, and improve my *MINDSET* for the next three years. It will be a challenging but incredible journey that we will all run together, right?

Afterword
Parting Thoughts

Adoptions to change are crucial in the 21 Century. But, of course, the baby boomers were familiar with the book "Who Moved My Cheese" and how it revealed the need to reinvent ourselves every time we change jobs. Or what about the day a new employer hires you is the same day you should be looking for your next job, as your job will not last for 30 years?

If your job requires you to produce daily social media videos, can you do it daily without excuses? Please don't say I'm from the old school; I don't know how. Can you set a 90-day window to master each innovative technology, if not in 21 days? Is it scripting that's holding you back? Do you need someone to help you write a script? Then ask someone to help you right away. Do you know how to answer objections or lead someone to make a decision script? Everyone is willing to help.

Are you afraid to make phone calls? Ask someone to help you to produce a script. It is all about scripting to raise your confidence, right? Can you put together an enormous number of face-to-face activities in 90 days? Be an audacious goal-setter. You don't need to meet with 5,000 families like I did in 90 days, but think of the amount of success you will have if you do, right?

Success in sales only comes to those who can quickly put in a substantial amount of activities. They then grow the foundation with a relationship goal after that, find out what problems exist and solve them for folks repeatedly, or ask people to repeat what they want and provide it for them. All of these require working hard constantly and continually improving your mindset.

How do folks show up on their first day on the job? How creative and solutions-oriented are you? How likely can you execute flawlessly over and over again? Where does one develop and improve communication skills, continue fostering innovative ideas, and build transferable habits to any roles, responsibilities, and circumstances without quitting? As an employer, do you know why the talent pool today is not that talented anymore?

I hope readers of this book will take on a habit of reading 20 minutes per day, watching 20 minutes of educational YouTube per day, starting a mastermind group with people above their ambition level, and meeting with them for five years. After all, you will be precisely the same person you are five years from now as you are today except for the books you read, the videos you watch, and the people you hang around with, right?

Twenty minutes per day is 121 hours per year. Right? Or three work weeks?

Here's to YOUR New Beginning in adopting existing ideas and telling one of your future employers you had done something 20 minutes every day for the last three months or three years, right?

If you ate a hamburger every day for 90 days, how would you feel, and how would you look? What if you eat a salad every day for 90 days? How would you feel, and how would you look? ... 20 minutes per day will make all the difference for you in 90 days, right?

Top 10 – New Habits to Adopt for 30 Days

1. Wake up and decide you will THRIVE today and for the rest of your day, no matter what happens. Be a Beacon of Hope to Others.
2. Listen to one Ted Talk per day
3. Eat some fruit with your lunch every day and again at dinner

4. Have ten conversations with prospective clients
5. Read a motivation book 20 minutes per day
6. Ask people close to you to help mentor you
7. Take $50 and buy an online coaching course and follow it for 30 days or get free coaching tips from any YouTube guru
8. Call up the Southwestern Company and offer to house college students over the summertime
9. Call a realtor and ask how to make money selling real estate; take the test and pass it
10. Call a loan officer and ask how to make money being a loan officer; take the test and pass it

If my stories have impacted you, I am in the home mortgage financing business. I continue to give my all as my Creator leads me. He put me on this path with our journeys together. #MeToWe. I am always looking for individuals and companies to share my vision of empowering foster children.

If you ever come across folks who are looking to buy or refinance a home, please let me know how I may be able to assist them as a #ProblemSolvingPro. I consult folks when they are going through a Divorce seeking to do an equity buyout, or buying a home before or after a divorce, with Reverse Mortgage for those 55 years or older; luxury home escrows always have challenges to solve along with educating first-time home buyers. I love educating folks and saving them time and money. Please refer me at:

www.JoeMortgageTeam.com

P.S. 30 days will pass whether you do something or not, right? It took 30 days to write the first draft of this book. So what will your bold, audacious goal be with hairs on it? What can you accomplish in the next 30 days?

*** Repetition *** Repetition *** Repetition ***

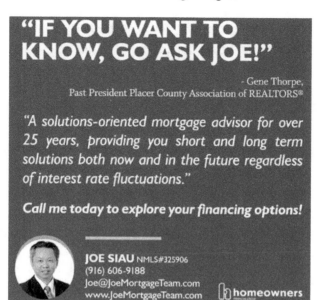

Painted by my wife, who has no art skills
20 minutes per day

www.paintwithnumber.com

About Joe Siau

From a passion for playing the trumpet at 12 to being a civil servant working at the Department of Defense for seven years and then Hewlett Packard for three years, Joe Siau has since built a very successful mortgage practice for over the next 21 years in Roseville, CA. Joe's worldwide business and cross-cultural perspectives have been his source for new and bold ideas, and Joe is not afraid to share how he capitalized on them by developing new work habits.

"Habits Driven is The Game Changer" was born with the assumption that everyone already knows it takes good habits to succeed in any endeavor.

Execution-wise, why are some people able to execute and succeed while others are not able to achieve and not able to grow? Joe has consistently performed very well in pursuing and scaling multiple entrepreneurial business ventures. So what are the questions we should be asking? Do you have great ideas? Are there missing ingredients in your pursuit? Do you have a solid work ethic and great habits?

How does the post covid teenager know what successful habits look like or smell like today? How do you collaborate and put ideas and practices to the best use for you, your family, and your community?

Joe Siau ranked as one of the Top 1% of Scotsman Guide Mortgage Originators in 2020 and 2021 amongst over 550,000 lenders in the United States. Joe always has excellent ideas and great habits. He is a daily subject matter expert in home mortgage financing and a #ProblemsSolvingPro.

You will enjoy the thoroughness of Joe's insights. You and your client will appreciate his work ethic and integrity. You can count on him as your friend and lender for life. Joe wrote and completed the first draft of this book in 30 days. He does what he says.

"Habits Driven is the Game Changer"
Habits will help you build muscle memories

~

As a paid or unpaid recipient of this book, can I ask you to extend your goodwill and provide at least two Five Stars reviews for:

Joe Mortgage Team or Habits Driven
@ Google page, Yelp, Amazon, Social Media, etc.

Credits

Edited and Formatted

by Kenneth L. Birks

Straight Arrow Publications

Ken@straitarrow.net
www.straitarrow.net

Cover Design

By Hans Bennewitz
design / illustration /art direction
hans@modedesign.us
www.hansbenewitz.com

Front Cover Photo

By Stephen Tse

Please Join the FaceBook Group

Game Changer for feedback